The Secrets I Share With My Friends

Conquering Fears to Create Masterpieces

By Nadine J. Larder

The Secrets I Share With Friends
Conquering Fears To Create Masterpieces

For information, visit www.NadineLarder.com

Cover Designed By:
Lisa Norton, Senior Designer at Printerbees.com

Photos By:
Steve Hardison and Nadine Larder

ISBN: 978-0-9960435-2-6

With Sincere Gratitude...

This book is dedicated to Allison Crow... my art and life coach. Allison introduced me to a part of myself I hadn't had the pleasure of meeting before. She introduced me to the artist in me that had been hiding in the shadows of my fear for the first 48 years of my life. She taught me how to let go and let the paint lead the way. She introduced me to intuitive art, art where the only rules are to "follow the feel good" and my intuition. I will be forever grateful for what working with her opened up in me. Had I not crossed paths with Allison, I'm not sure I would have ever met this part of myself. Had I not hired Allison to be my coach, my life might not have taken me down this road. One of the most amazing roads I've ever traveled.

Thank you from the depths of my heart and soul for your contribution to my life Allison. Thank you for showing up as your authentic self and for helping me to know more of my authentic self. I love you dearly and my gratitude for you is never ending.

~Nadine

The Man in the Arena

"It is not the critic who counts; not the man who points out how the strong man stumbles, or where the doer of deeds could have done them better. The credit belongs to the man who is actually in the arena, whose face is marred by dust and sweat and blood; who strives valiantly; who errs, who comes short again and again, because there is no effort without error and shortcoming; but who does actually strive to do the deeds; who knows great enthusiasms, the great devotions; who spends himself in a worthy cause; who at the best knows in the end the triumph of high achievement, and who at the worst, if he fails, at least fails while daring greatly, so that his place shall never be with those cold and timid souls who neither know victory nor defeat."

An excerpt from a speech Theodore Roosevelt gave in 1910.

When I heard Brene Brown read it for the first time I cried as she read it because it resonated with me so deeply. Mr. Roosevelt was talking about me in that speech... "The "man" in the arena getting my butt kicked because I actually choose to get IN the arena, facing my fears head on, staring at them, accepting them, acknowledging them, naming them and feeling them as I risk failing. As I risk falling on my face, only so can I get up and try again. And it's likely as scary for me as it is for you. My fear is no different than the next person, sometimes it can be debilitating, keeping me from starting as you'll read in the pages of this journal. Sometimes we just have to power through to do and experience what calls, when it calls because it's the call that's only meant to be answered by one person.

I kept this journal as I powered through the largest (and scariest) project of my life! I was as scared as one can be to decide to take it on. I had to say "yes" when asked if I was interested in doing it because I knew this special project was meant for me and only me. My intuition told me it would be magical and miraculous, yet scary as I ventured in to the unknown.

I kept this journal so I'd never forget how it felt to be on this journey.

Before you read my journal, I should provide you with some background on where it all started.

In June of 2012, my husband and I moved our family from California to Arizona. It was decision based on troubled finances and escaping the high cost of living in the Bay Area that left us buried in debt to the tune of 1.2 million dollars.

The details of how we got there and how we turned it around are in my book, *The Secrets I Share With My Friends Life Lessons From An Imperfect Woman*. It's quite a story!

While finances were at the core, I also had a strong sense that Arizona was where I NEEDED to be. Almost like there was something waiting for me there that wasn't available to me in California. I can't describe it, but it was strong and I was right!

It took about two years to financially recover and get back on our feet again. My business was doing well, my husband had a great job and I decided it was time to hire myself a coach. A life coach. I'm a huge fan of coaching, I've experienced tremendous growth in the past when working with coaches.

I'm very spiritual so I decided the best way to find a coach was to simply ask God to send me one. So I stepped in to the courtyard outside my office, lifted my hands up and asked God to send me a coach. My faith and my ability to manifest thoughts in to things is tremendous, so I knew I needed to be VERY specific in what I wanted. I told Him that I didn't want just any coach, I wanted the best one on the planet! It was a tall order but I knew if anyone could help me find the coach meant for me, it was Him.

I put the request out and didn't give it much thought after that.

It wasn't two weeks later that a man named Steve Hardison walked up to me in a parking garage and introduced himself.

He wasn't a life coach, he was The Ultimate Coach and I can remember it like it was yesterday.

His energy was different than anything I had ever felt before. There was something about him that was unexplainable. Something that felt pure and authentic. I experienced his aura as so light and bright white, it was almost blinding. Electric... yet so calm, centered, authentic and beautiful. Trust me, there's a reason people ask to hear the story of how you met Steve once they know you've encountered him. The stories are always fascinating no matter who is telling it. Jody Vehr has one of the best "meeting Steve stories." It's detailed in her book *Just Hit Send*. I love her story!

When Steve and I met, we were both attending a business conference in Phoenix put on by Infusionsoft. I was headed to my car with my team and he was headed to his.

It was the InfusionSoft conference two years prior that initially brought me to Arizona. My husband and I moved our family here after I attended the 2012 conference because I loved it so much and felt called to be here.

Steve was a VIP guest of Clate Mask, the CEO of Infusionsoft. He was Clate's coach. I was there to accept a marketing award and as one of the conference speakers. I was also releasing my first book that very day, a business book called *The Secrets I Share With My Friends Everything I Know About Building A Small Business.*

We spoke briefly, mostly small talk, I invited him to my session the following day, and he left. He returned a few moments later, pulling up along side us in his car. He had come back to share gifts! He hopped out of the car, opened his trunk and proceeded to give each of us a book written by Steve Chandler. His only request was that we not to take a book we wouldn't read. I was excited and appreciative. I love to read and these titles were right up my alley! Steve Chandler is a brilliant author!

Because I was releasing my book that day, I asked if I could reciprocate and give him my new book. He asked what it was about before he accepted to make sure it was something he'd actually read. Me being me, I jokingly said to him "don't take what you're not going to read." We laughed and he promised he'd read it. He said "I am my word and I will definitely read it, you have my word." I knew he was sincere and I knew he was telling me the truth. I could feel it.

Before he left he asked me to sign the book and it was then that I learned he was a coach, he told me he was Clate's coach. He also asked if I knew who Iyanla Vanzant was because he was her coach too. I'm a raving fan of Iyanla Vanzant and Clate's business (Infusionsoft) changed my business and my life! I absolutely knew about both of them. I couldn't believe he just walked up to me and introduced himself.

When we parted ways in the parking garage that afternoon, I knew I had just experienced a special moment, a moment in my life I would reflect back on. I knew something had changed and I knew I was meant to meet that man! The Ultimate Coach, Steve Hardison. God always comes through for me.

I felt so sure about this man, I became a "Clate Mask stalker" at the conference for the sole purpose of asking him about his coach Steve. This is not something I would do normally and it's a huge conference, how would I even find him!?!? I finally cornered him later that evening while he was leaving VIP party I was also attending. I was literally the very last person to leave the party. I was so intent on learning more. When I asked him about Steve, everything about his energy shifted. He paused calmly, looked at me and said "So, you met Steve?" He said it as if he knew what I had experienced.

It was in that moment talking to Clate that I knew Steve was the coach sent for me. I didn't know how I would make it happen, but I KNEW it was no accident we had met in the parking garage earlier that day.

It would be a year of praying, meditating, manifesting, focusing and great miracles that lead to me becoming one of Steve's clients. It was as life changing and amazing as I knew it would be. Steve goes all in with his clients and what an honor it is for me to have been one of them. As Iyanla Vanzant says "*If I had one gift I could give to every human being on the planet it would be to have a coaching experience with Steve Hardison*" I fully agree!

My coaching with Steve was as miraculous as our meeting in the parking garage and it was only the beginning of what we would create together.

There's a reason Steve has clients who routinely fly in to Phoenix from all over the world to coach with him in his most sacred space, his office. If you want to coach with Steve, he only coaches in person and he only coaches in his office.

Oh how I love this man and what he does and creates with his mind, energy, spirit and everything he has. A true life force.

In November of 2016, I began manifesting and praying, asking God to help me once again. I put my request out in to the world via my journal. Declaring and owning the fact that "I am an artist who is paid well for the art I create." I had been doing a lot of painting and my artwork was well received by many of the people who saw it when I posted it on social media. I made a decision that it was time to get serious about selling my art. It was time to accept that "I am an artist." It was time to stop the limited thinking and overcome the fear of stepping in to the light.

I had some limiting stories that my ego had me believing which kept me hidden. The story I'd told myself since I was a child. "*I can't draw, I can't paint, I don't do that kind of art, I can barely draw a stick figure!*" After careful consideration, I can honestly tell you that my fear of failing kept me from even trying. That story was something I made up. I'd never even tried to draw or sketch anything more complicated than a stick figure! It was a made up story to keep me from risking failure. It was a made up story that kept me from helping my kids with their art homework assignments. I didn't want to let them down with my lack of ability because I KNEW I couldn't do it! I didn't possess those skills. I honestly had no clue I had any ability to create art on a canvas. It was a part of myself I hadn't had the pleasure of meeting yet.

I lied to myself until I was 49 years old when art came calling for me. I became fascinated with art in 2015 in a way it had never interested me before. I became fascinated as a result of a woman named Allison Crow. She is an intuitive artist and life coach who holds painting retreats and works with private clients, a true creative. I loved her art, it spoke to me and studying her and her art made me want to see more art! I spent hours and hours on Pinterest looking at her art along with any other art I could find that was interesting to me. I became familiar with what I liked and what I didn't, much like when you're tasting wine. I couldn't stop, I was obsessed, it was calling me.

Before I knew it, I had signed up for a wine and paint event with a friend. It was in the safe confines of a fool proof painting and an instructor to guide me through my fears. I'd never painted before and this felt safe to me. I painted for the first time on May 20, 2015.

At that painting party I learned how to move paint on a canvas, how to hold a paintbrush, I learned about adding water and I learned about blending colors on the canvas. Just as I had seen and loved in some of Allison's art! I dipped my toe in the water and the water was perfect, enticing and inviting.

I continued to study and look at art. I began to watch painting tutorials, to pay attention to brush marks, to notice the movement of the paint, the colors, the contrast... all of it. I couldn't get enough and so I began to play with paint.

I put some paint on a canvas and kept playing with it, not knowing what I was painting. I just kept adding paint and decided to see what would happen. I decided to be brave and

risk seeing if it would become anything. Allison had talked about trusting the process, playing with the paint and letting intuition lead the way. I did what she said and I created my first original piece. The Tree Of Life.

I later hired Allison to be my coach I was so drawn to her, her energy, her creativity, her intuition, her art. She coached me on painting, she helped me to understand following my intuition, she gave me assignments. It was a beautiful experience, a tremendous gift to my creativity, to my ... SELF. . .and to "*who I be*." I love Allison dearly and I LOVED coaching with her. What a blessing she continues to be in my life.

I enjoyed painting so much and my art was so appreciated and encouraged when I shared it on social media that I dared myself to put my intuition to the test. I decided to try painting live on Facebook and allow the people watching to paint with me, to be involved in the process. It felt incredibly vulnerable and risky, but I felt drawn to give it a try and see what would happen. We created amazing art together, and "International Paint Party" was born! People from all over the world join me to paint and participate, it's incredibly fun.

Little did I know that Steve Hardison had been watching me paint on Facebook Live and tuning in to my "International Paint Party." He loved my art. He loved the Tree of Life painting hanging in his office that I gifted him for his 60th birthday. He told me how much he loved it when I gifted it to him, but those old stories kept me from 1000% believing he wasn't just being kind and gracious as the receiver of a gift, one that I made.

I can now honestly say he was 100,000% sincere in how much he loved my art. The only one not believing in me, was me with those old tapes playing in the back of my mind. I learned a valuable lesson about conquering fear and not believing the life limiting BS stories we make up so we don't have to "get in the ring."

Now that you have a little background on where our story started, how I met Steve and how art came looking for me, I hope you enjoy my journal of the creation of The 11:11 Masterpiece Wall.

The meaning of 11:11

"11:11 is the Universe knocking itself out to give you evidence of your alignment." ~ Abraham Hicks

It's believed by many 11:11 is an angel number related to the concept of synchronicity. When we notice the number 1111, it's thought to be an invitation to "wake-up" and pay attention to the way things in life are lining up perfectly to serve us. A reminder that the Universe is always working in our favor and that things are always unfolding perfectly.

It can also be seen as a key to unlock the subconscious mind, and remind us that we are spiritual beings having a physical experience, rather than physical beings embarking upon spiritual experiences.

12-6-2016

Today my life took at turn when I received a message from Steve Hardison at 11:00 pm asking if I was awake and able to call if I was. I was awake... so I called.

It was on this day he told me he'd been paying attention to me and my art on Facebook. He told me how much he loved my art, that it spoke to him. He invited me to paint a mural of my art in his back yard on a wall he described as large. Large doesn't begin to describe its size!

He posed this question to me at precisely 11:11 p.m.

The 11:11 Masterpiece Wall was born on 12-6-2016 at 11:11 p.m.

I didn't sleep that night ... I couldn't believe it was real! Was this really happening???

The journey of it being created is in the pages of this detailed journal I kept while creating and painting this amazing masterpiece.

12-7-2016

I responded at precisely 11:11 a.m. saying I wanted to accept the job and discuss it further.

Steve

I have no words to describe how moved I am by your words and by your invitation to paint and create my art on your wall. My dream of having my art be "known" being so much closer to reality. My thoughts have been consumed since last night by what will potentially go on that wall! I'm absolutely giddy beyond measure. Tuning into my intuition and the images that come to mind when I consider the magic created in your office. I knew when I put out to God that I wanted to be paid to do art it would happen quickly... I just never imagined this! Thank God I also pray a lot about what comes out when I paint... I pray for continued inspiration to paint something that means something to someone. I can't wait to meet and discuss further. Let me know what

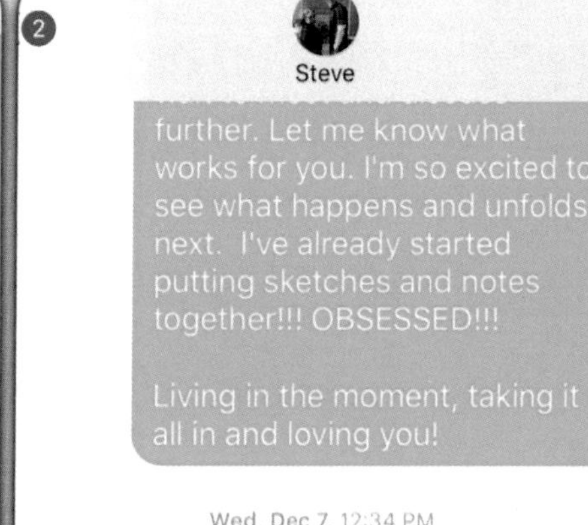

2

Steve

further. Let me know what works for you. I'm so excited to see what happens and unfolds next. I've already started putting sketches and notes together!!! OBSESSED!!!

Living in the moment, taking it all in and loving you!

Wed, Dec 7, 12:34 PM

I am so excited for us. Let me give you a few optional times that we can meet here at Thee Wall; Thee Canvas; The Embryonic Masterpiece: this Friday at 10 am, Wednesday the 14th at 10am, Friday the 16th at 2pm. If those times do not work we could meet most evenings at 5 pm as long as we have a little light. Please confirm when it is convenient so I can plan accordingly. Loving you and your passion. Blessings to you. SFH

12-9-2016

I was hired!!! Today I met with Steve at the 11:11 Masterpiece Wall. It's HUGE!!!

I accepted the project, I'm being compensated nicely and I have the greatest boss ever!

Feeling both excited and completely overwhelmed!

What have I gotten myself in to? I've never painted anything larger than a canvas of 30 X 40 inches! This entire wall is 600 square feet!

Steve chose what he wanted on the wall from several canvases I brought with me as samples of my work. And so the journey begins…

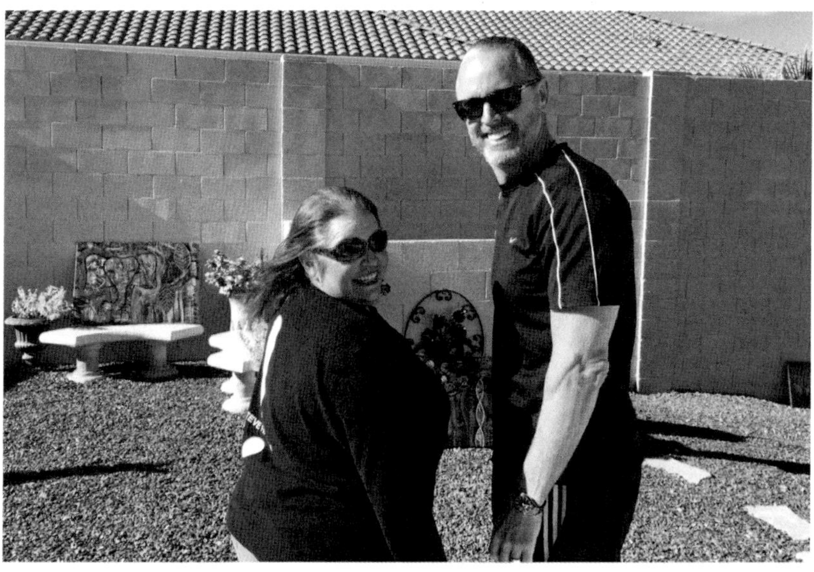

As an intuitive artist, I don't ever know what I'm painting or what will happen when I sit down in front of my easel and begin applying paint to my canvas. I follow the paint and the canvas to wherever it takes me. The outcome is a surprise and the creating of it, a journey.

I always infuse energy in to my art by painting inspiring words and messages on the base layer of each canvas. I like to begin with good energy to help move my art in the right direction. With The 11:11 Masterpiece Wall, I suggested to Steve that we do something similar to his wall… but that I wouldn't be the one to write the words this time. I suggested this time my "canvas" could have the energy infused in to it with words put there by his clients, friends and family.

I was thinking about words… simple words, like "love, happiness, gratitude, dream, God, achievement, family, etc. etc." Steve had something completely different in mind… which blew my mind!

He planned to have all of his clients and family write the declarations of who they are and what they stand for on the wall. He would reserve the wall where The Tree Of Life was to be painted for his family and only his family would write there. Sounded like a solid plan to me.

Let the freaking out begin! Because I've never done anything like this before, I have to learn how to paint a mural. The encouragement from friends has been overwhelming and comforting. I have tremendous gratitude for the support! I've been mentally consumed with learning everything I can about how to paint a mural and have the paint stick to the wall so it's there as long as possible! Forever if I have it my way.

My Notes....

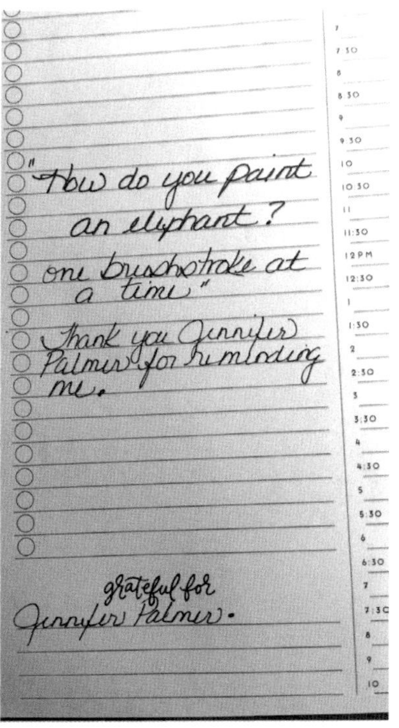

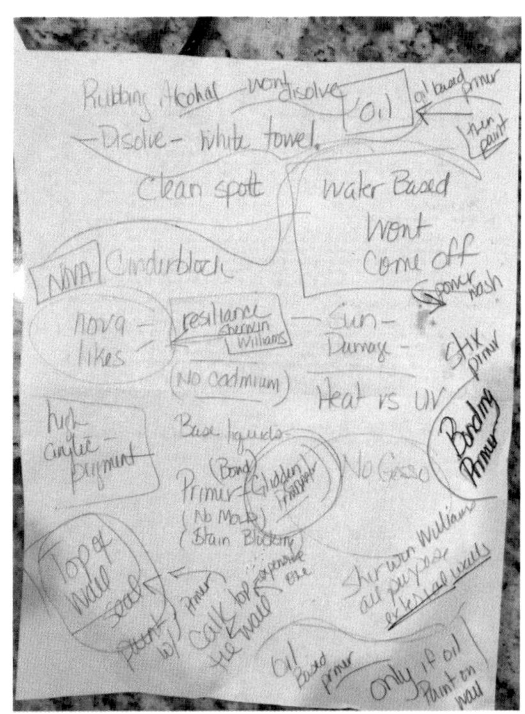

12-17-16

Step 1… Prep the wall for priming.

Power wash wall with Tom's help and Steve always cheering me on! The support is amazing.

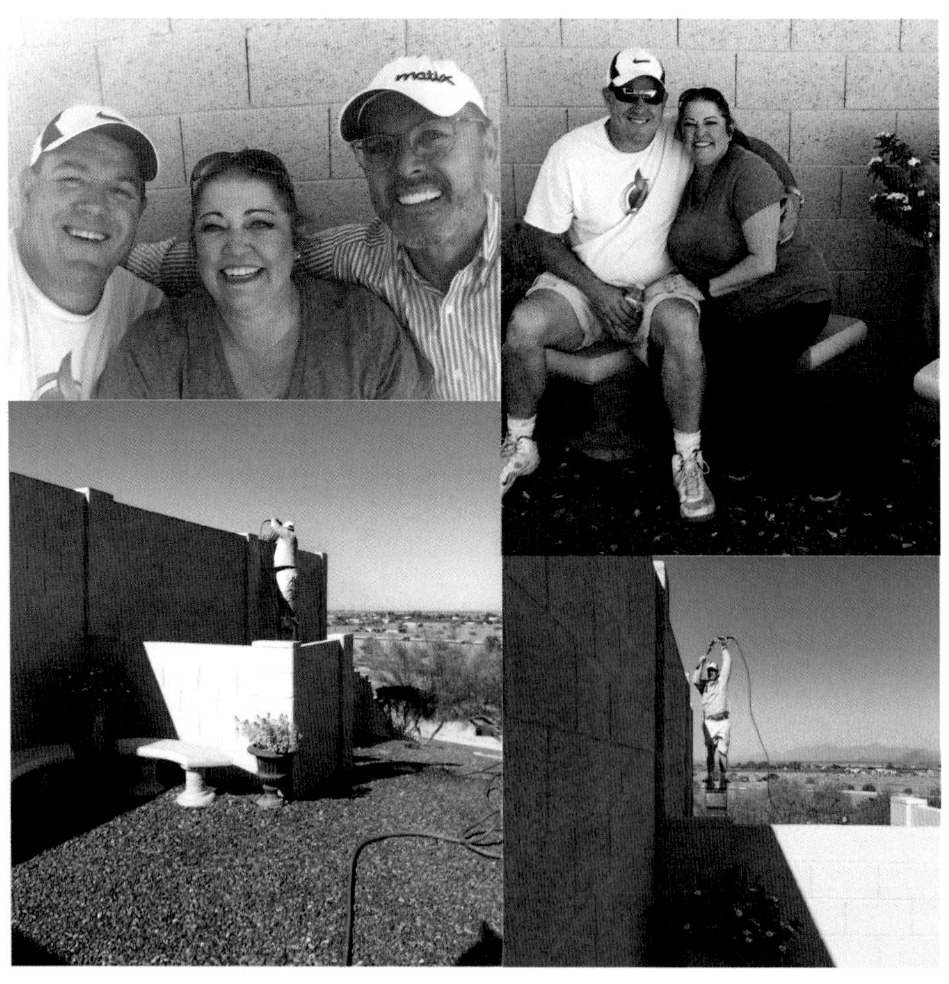

1-5-2016

Step 2…
Primer! So thankful to have Tom's help spraying the primer on the wall.

This would be our second trip to prime the wall. The first time we came to do it, the sprayer broke.

1-2-2017

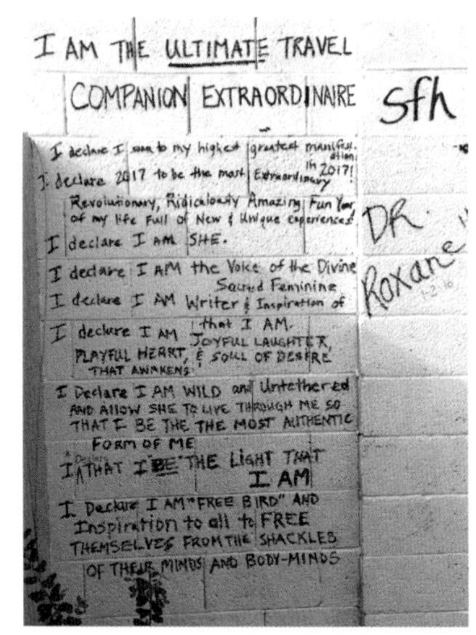

I received a call from Steve letting me know Dr. Roxane Beck was writing her declarations of who she is on the wall. She was writing where Phoenix Rising will go. She once had a business called The Phoenix. So fitting. She has big dreams and I'm appreciative of what she put on the wall.

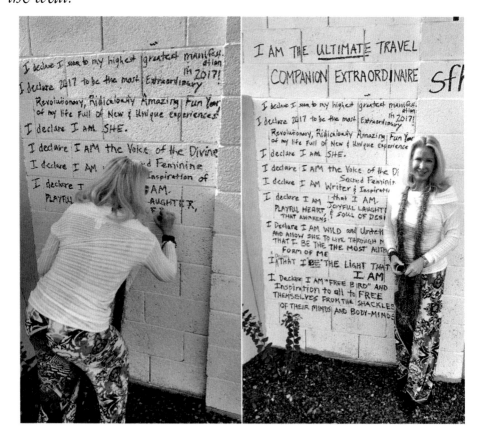

1-2-17

Steve called to let me know Clate Mask was writing on the wall. He was on a ladder. He promised to send photos.

I'm in awe of what's happening. I can't wait to see what Clate creates. His business has had such a profound impact on me. My life is what it is because Infusionsoft granted me my freedom. Im forever grateful for Clate's dream and Steve's support in creating it. It gave birth to dreams I didn't even know I had.

Simply miraculous full circle moment of a lifetime.

God is good.

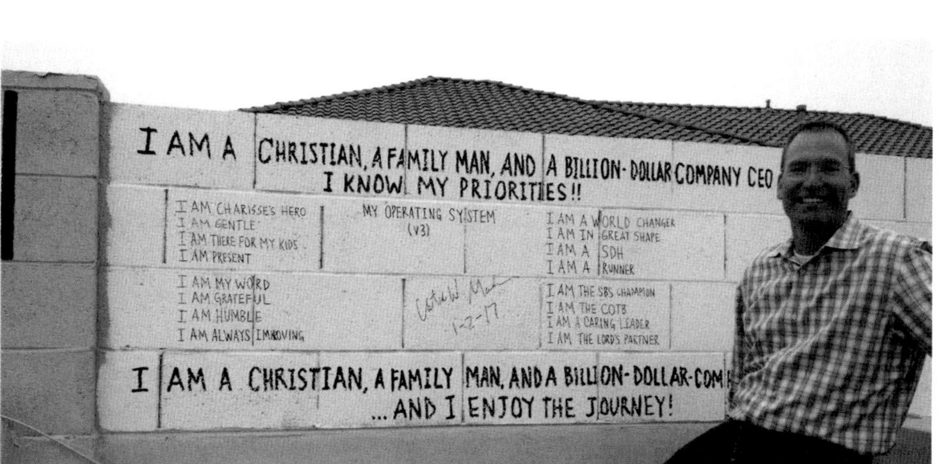

1-2-2017

A World Famous
ARTIST
is being born

I can feel it!

I am an artist

Oh My Gosh!!!!

1-6-2017

The Tree of Life wall has been reserved for The Hardison Family to sign. Steve was the first to write the declaration of who he is, followed by Amy. What they've written is beautiful, filled with love, passion, Christ, wisdom and so much more. I look forward to being in the presence of what is there and taking it in with all that I have.

It's beauty is beyond words.

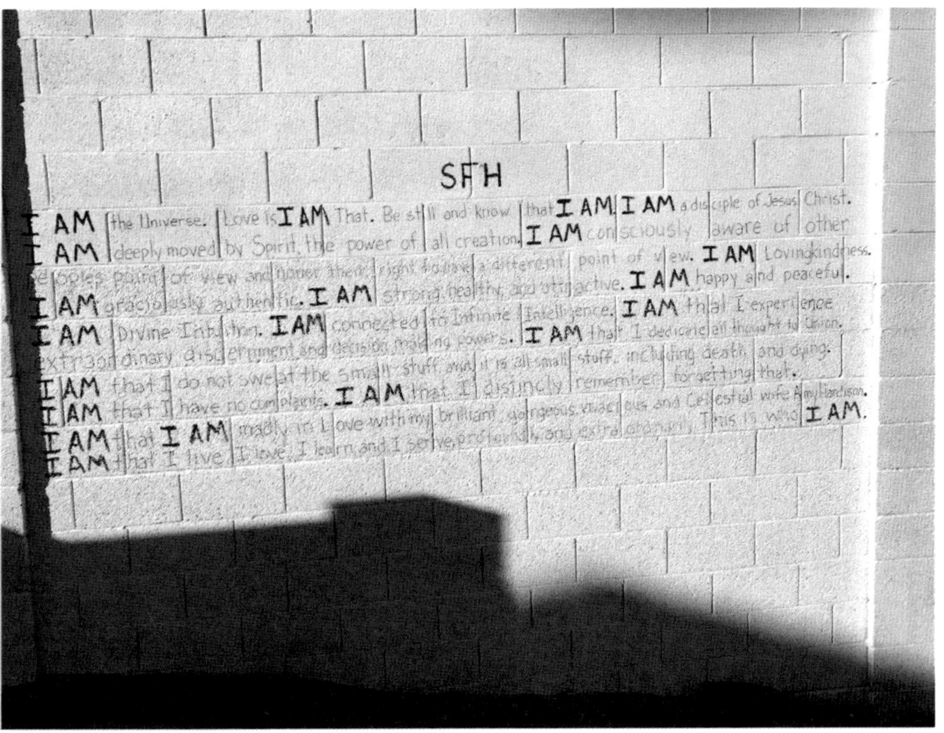

1-6-2017

When I received a text from Steve with his declarations on the wall… I cried.

I cried because I was so moved to see it on the wall. He's shared the declaration of who he is with me many times when I was blessed to coach with him. This time was different. I cried because this is the man I'm working for.

It's an absolute representation of him, as I've always experienced him. How can I not continue to grow being in his presence?

Trust me… Steve Hardison rubs off on you!!!!!

Amy Hardison's declaration is also so beautiful.

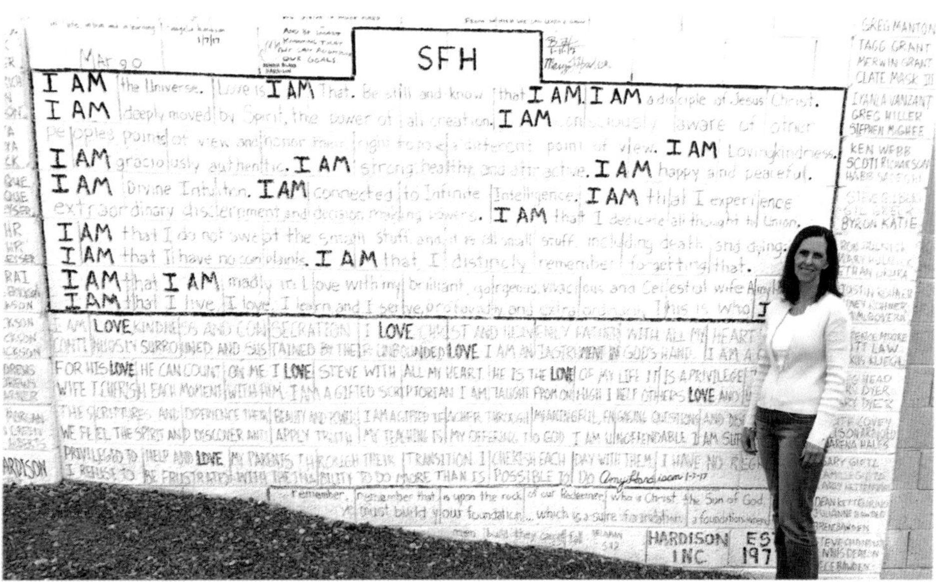

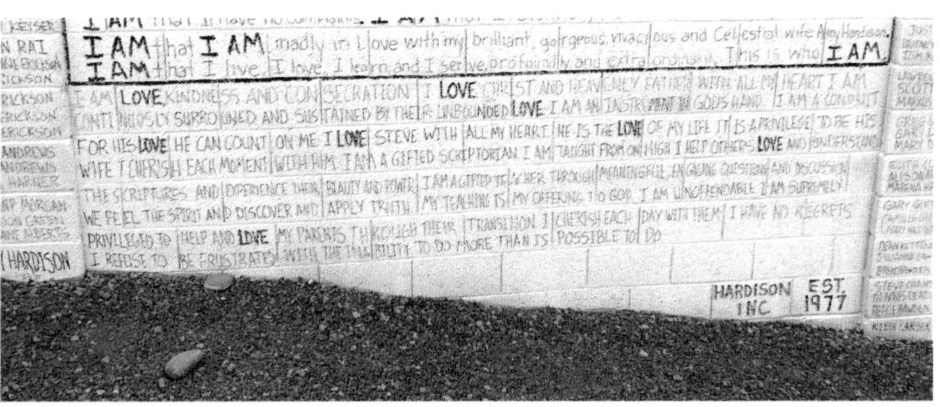

1-7-17

Clint Hardison and his wife Angela added their declarations statements. Absolutely beautiful. I read this out loud with Steve. I cried as I read it, I was so moved by what I read. Clint and Angela's daughter Margo signed her name to the wall too!

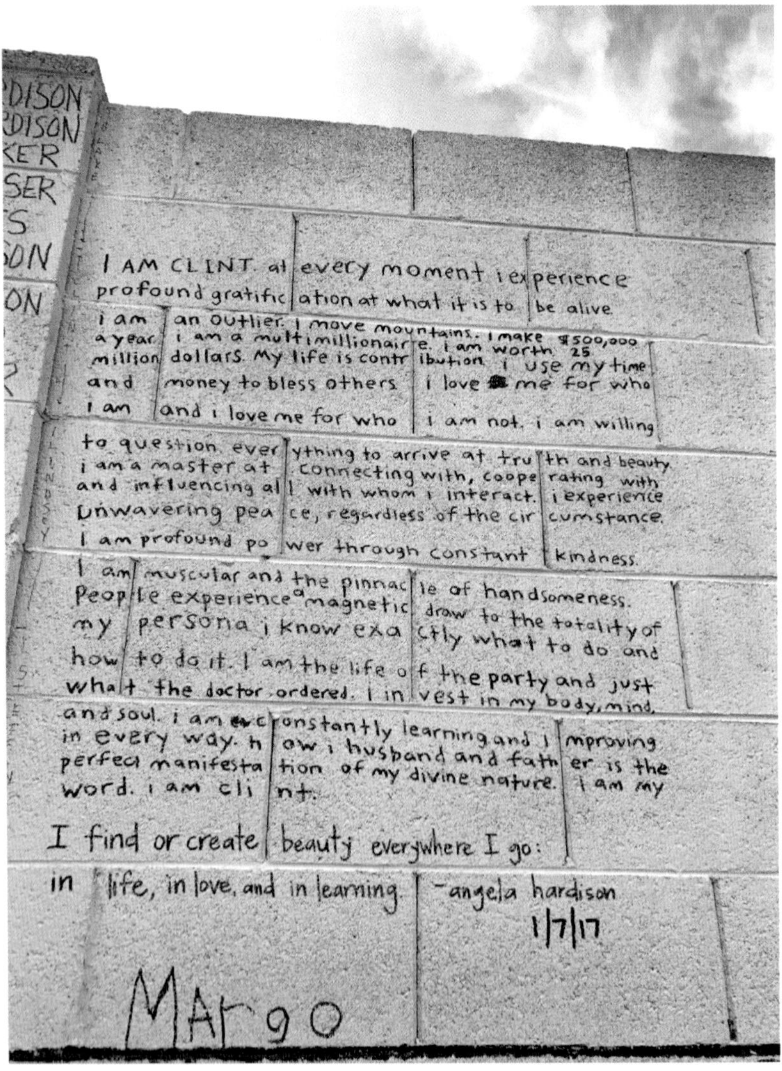

1-7-2017

I was shocked and awed to learn Steve spent the entire day writing the names of every person he's ever worked with on the pillars of the wall. I believe there are over 400 names, including my own on the pillars of the wall.

Amazing!!!!

1-8-2017

Today I was blessed to meet Deuce Lutui when he went to write his declaration on the wall. He is a most beautiful soul. Steve told me Deuce is one of the most spiritual people he's ever met. He lives his internal commitment every day. That is his life. TBOLITNFL right where the elephant painting "The Matriarch" will go. How fitting.

1-8-2017

The 11:11 Masterpiece Wall is evolving and looking amazing. Like I noted before… I was thinking about adding words… Steve had something entirely different and soooooo much more impactful in mind.

Many people asked if I would be signing the wall as one of Steve's clients. Steve's answer was simple…

The entire masterpiece is my signature.

1-8-2017

Karan Rai signed the wall with his declaration statement. He is the president of ADS out of Virginia. I am amazed at the number of people who travel across the country to meet with Steve. I can't begin to imagine what is created in Steve's sacred space… his office. Having spent my own time in this office, it's a pretty magical place.

Experiencing and reading what clients and family have written on the wall is truly amazing.

The quality of people and the declarations of who they are, what they stand for is beyond words. I read what people are committed to in their lives and the photos come to me via text and it's so inspiring. Filled with the perfect type of energy to host the art I will create on top of it.

So amazing to witness. Even more amazing to be a part of.

1-8-2017

Karan Rai adding his declaration to the wall.

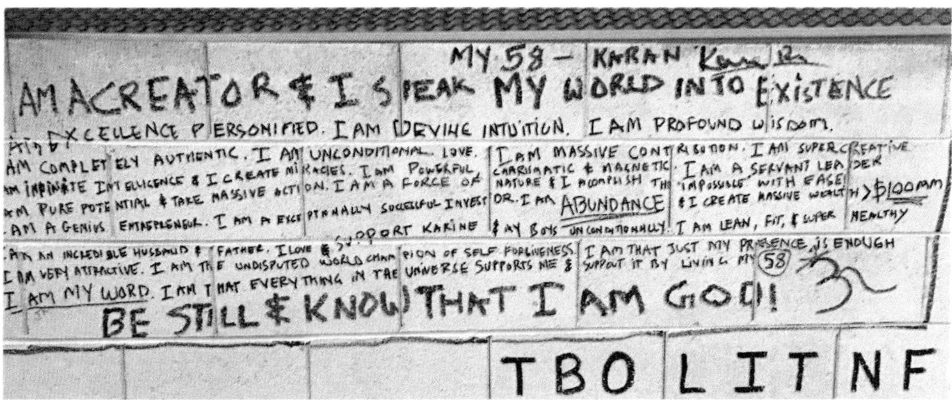

Karan's son K J Raj has his declaration on the wall too!

1-9-2017

Abigail Olaya, co-owner of the Venue at the Grove in Phoenix; added her beautiful energy and declaration to the wall. Simply beautiful

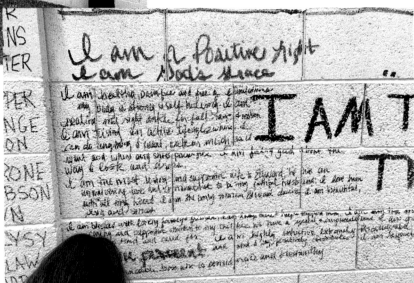

1-9-2017

Everyday is like Christmas!!! But better!

The photos of people writing on the wall keep showing up in text messages from Steve as I watch the The 11:11 Masterpiece Wall come alive with love and so many beautiful words.

I continue to be amazed at what I'm witnessing.

I think .. "why me?"

Then I remind myself "why not me?!?!"

I've got this!

This is truly amazing!

1-10-2017

Gina Carlson - Shakti has commitment! She was out past dark writing on the wall. Can't wait to see it in person! She said she listened to me painting on Facebook Live while she was writing. So exciting!

1-11-17

Blake Hardison, his wife Maryn and their adorable son Jonah writing "The Hardison Family Constitution" on the family wall where "The Tree of Life" will be.

A beautiful and inspiring read!

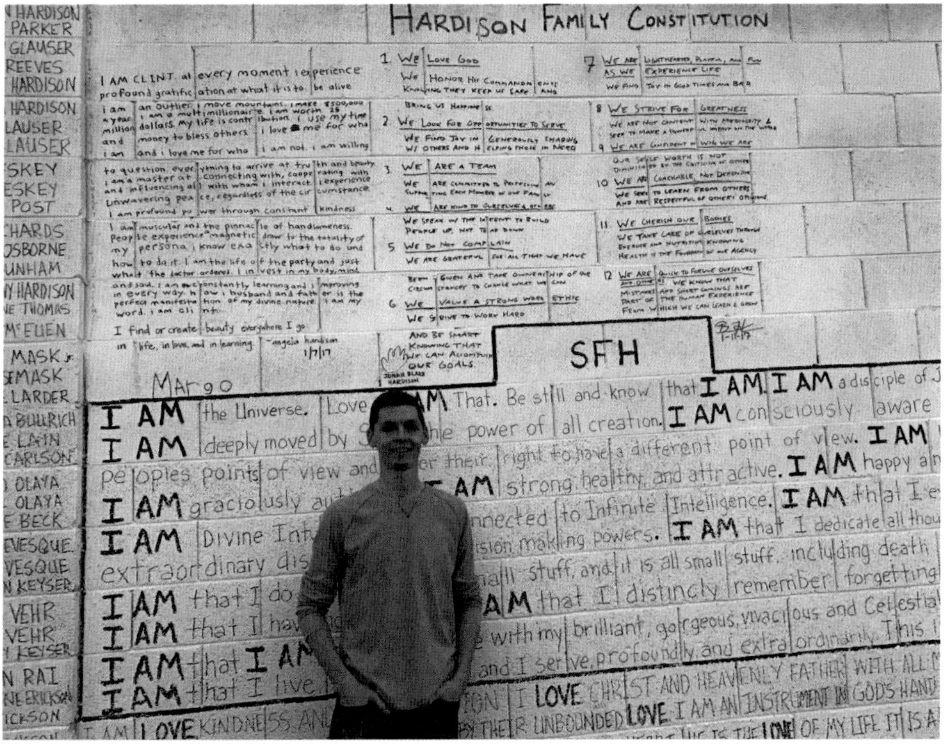

1-11-17

Deanna Chesley, who I've had the absolute pleasure of meeting sharing her declaration at the wall. 11:11 is very special to her.

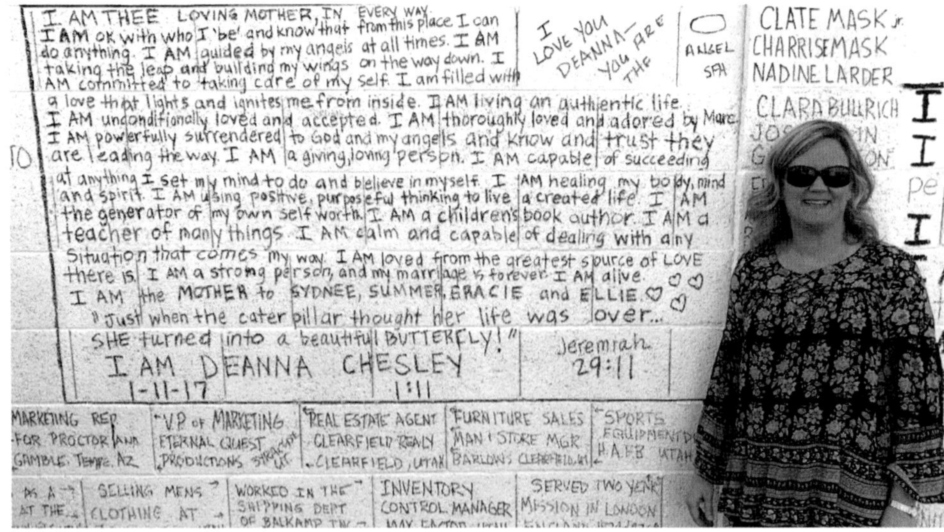

1-11-17

I absolutely love this photo of Jonathan Keyser! Love his theme! I hope to have the opportunity to meet Jonathan after reading this.

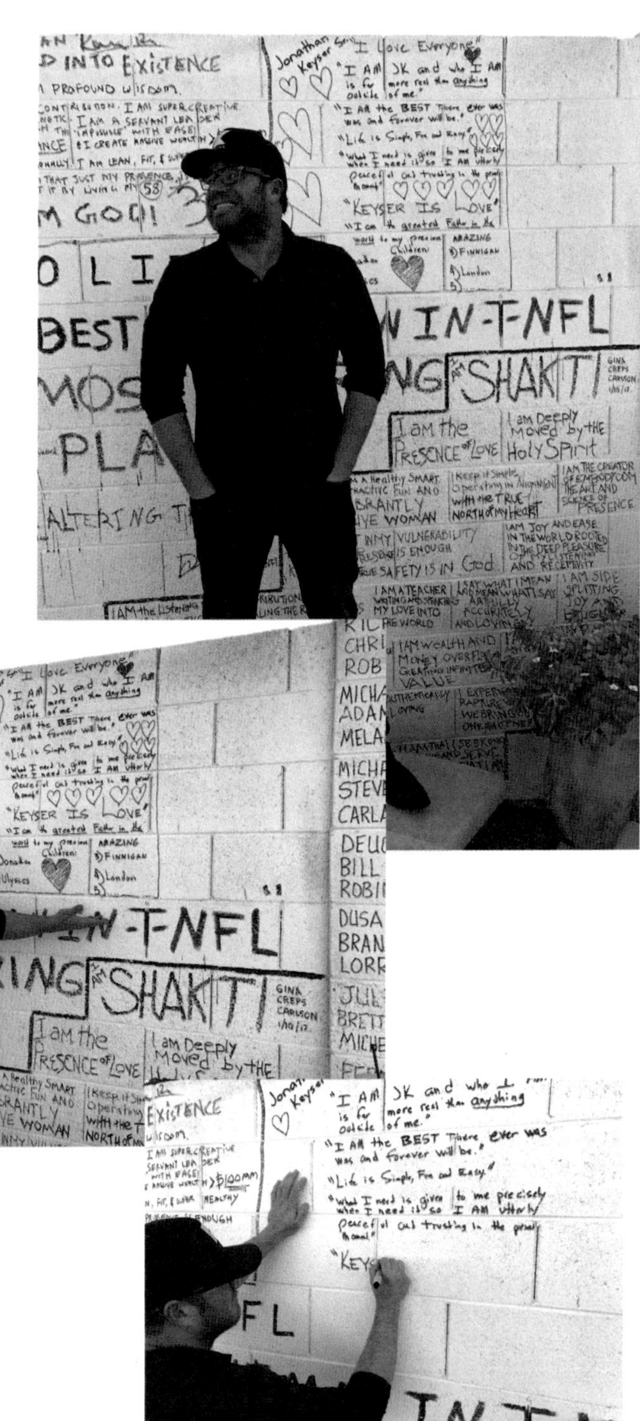

1-11-17

Kim Levesque, with her "To Love and Be Loved" creation.

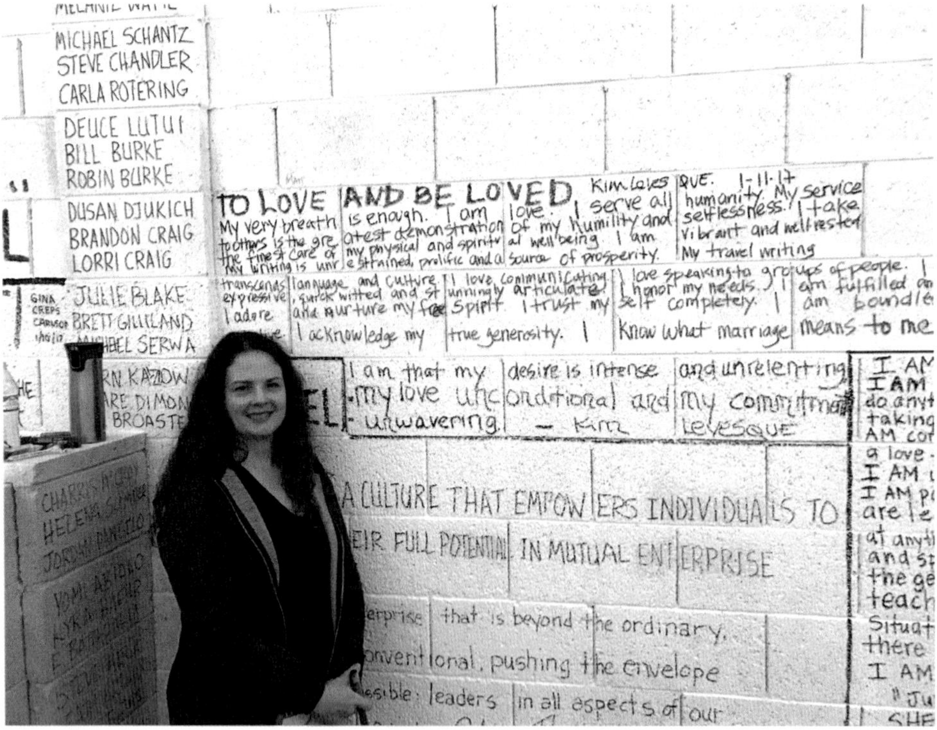

1-11-17

Matt Levesque, VP of World Wide Technologies writing his "Birthright" . . . in the dark! Now that's commitment. Matt's wife Kim held the light for him while he wrote on the wall. Teamwork!

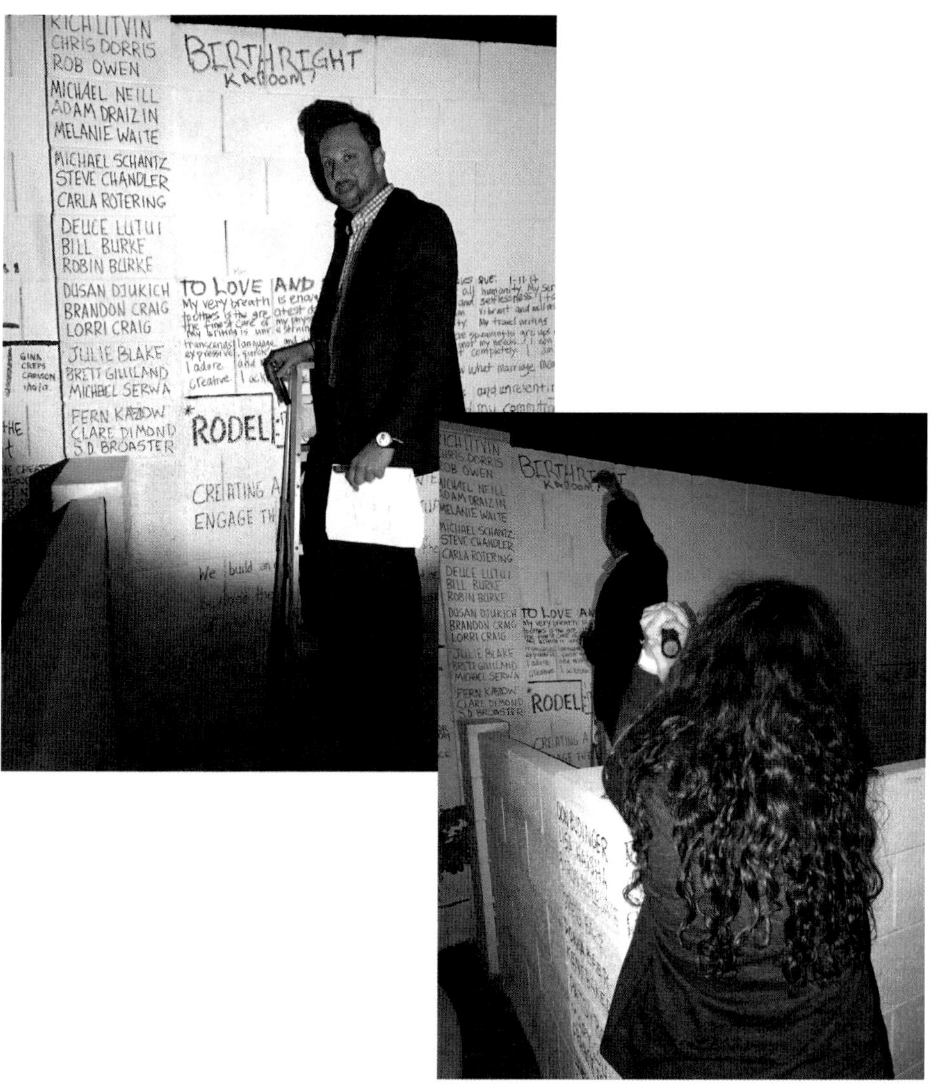

1-11-17

Blake Hardison of Keyser has two spots on the wall. One for his family and one that represents who he is and what he is committed to professionally.

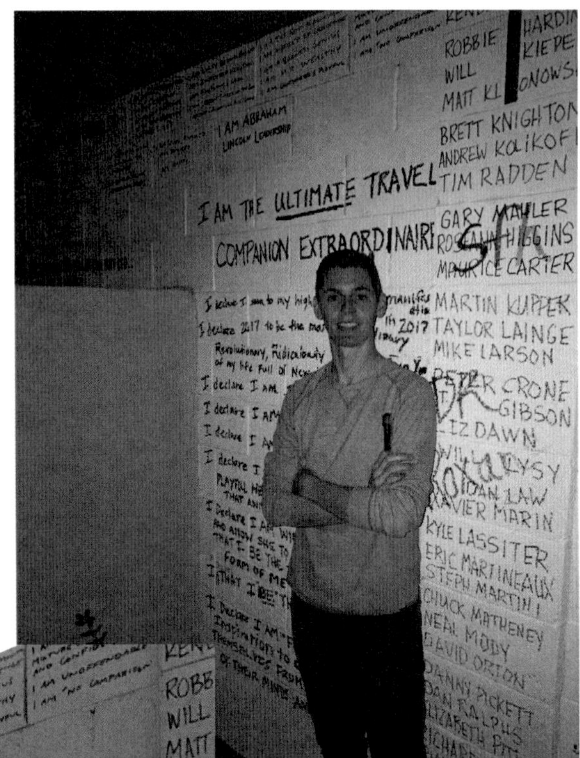

1-12-17

John D. Vehr Owner of Timney USA and Aviation Direct writing his "Manifesto on the Abundance of Love." Beautiful.

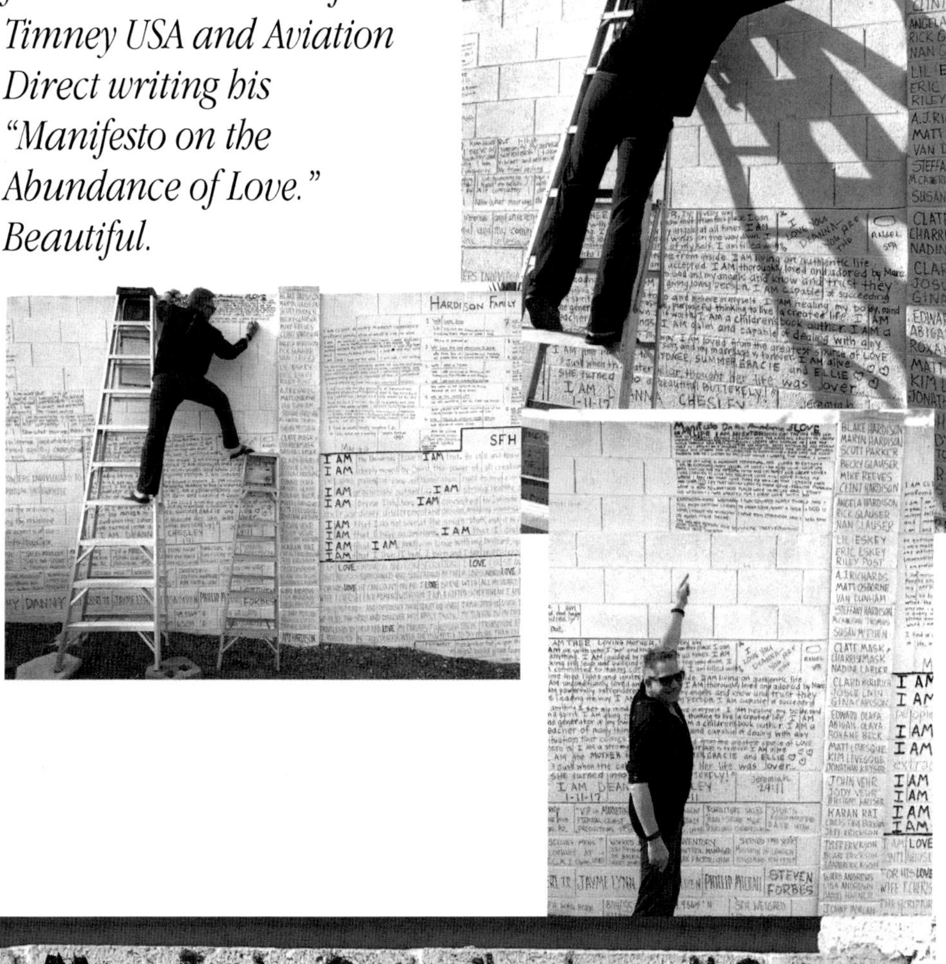

1-12-17

The wall continues to change and evolve as Steve's clients and family add their words and beautiful energy to the place I will eventually paint. What an amazing journey this is already and I haven't even started painting yet.

John Vehr and his dog Maisie.

1-12-2017

Jody Vehr, author of "Just Hit Send" writing "A Promise of the Heart" on the 11:11 canvas. "A Promise of the Heart" can be found in her book "Just Hit Send." An amazing story about her journey, her husband John Vehr and Steve Hardison. As Steve says… "What the "Serenity Prayer" is to alcoholics, "A Promise of the Heart" is to those creating power relationships." I agree having read it.

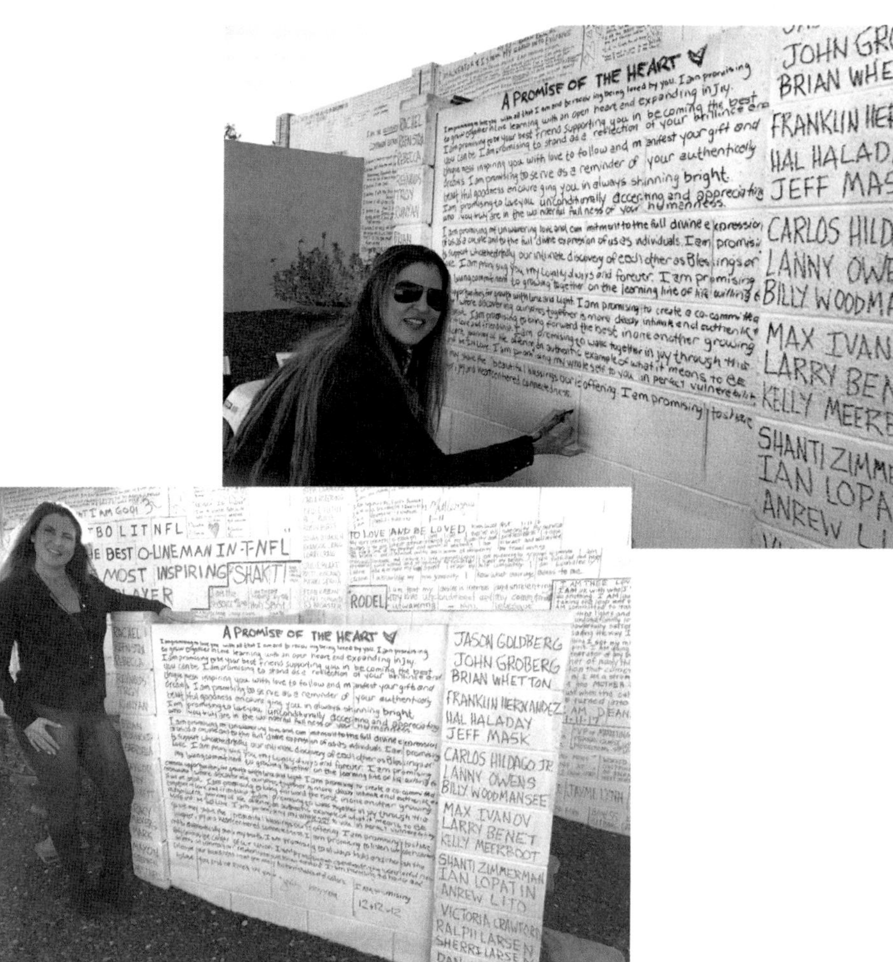

1-12-17

Jody also shared her "Eternal Prayer," which can also be found in her book "Just Hit Send." It's beautiful.

1-13-2017
A text message I sent to Steve as I step in to this amazing journey I'm on, unsure of where it will take me, keeping the faith.

I'm not sure what is happening, what God wants from me, but I will continue on this journey, stepping in to the light, allowing His light to shine through me and most of all I will have complete faith that He will carry me though to do the work I'm intended to.

I had to share because I feel like I'm not at all alone on this journey, that you're walking beside me and guiding me through. A gift from God.

"I am an artist that touches people around the world with my story, my art and my expression. I am the best at what I do, my light shines so bright it's almost blinding as does my authenticity and my brilliance. I show people the light that is God and I live the greatest expression of the life gifted to me by God. I treasure every moment and I remain present. I am Nadine... I am Hope."

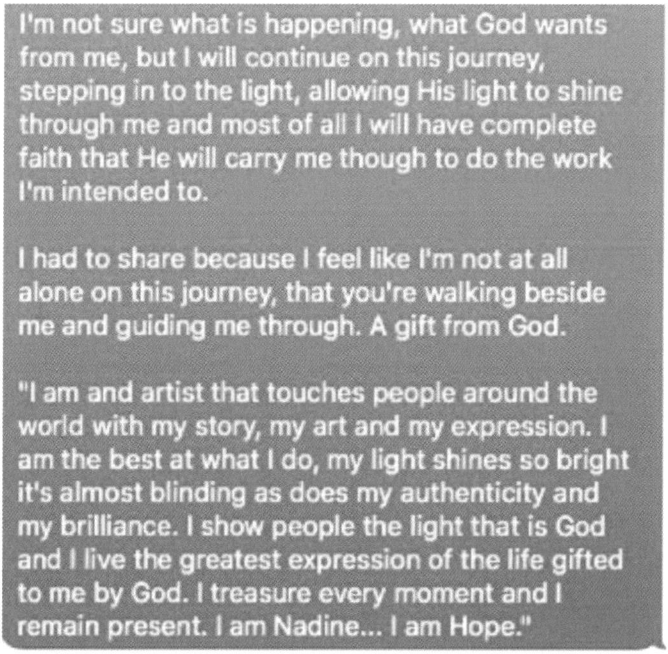

I'm not sure what is happening, what God wants from me, but I will continue on this journey, stepping in to the light, allowing His light to shine through me and most of all I will have complete faith that He will carry me though to do the work I'm intended to.

I had to share because I feel like I'm not at all alone on this journey, that you're walking beside me and guiding me through. A gift from God.

"I am and artist that touches people around the world with my story, my art and my expression. I am the best at what I do, my light shines so bright it's almost blinding as does my authenticity and my brilliance. I show people the light that is God and I live the greatest expression of the life gifted to me by God. I treasure every moment and I remain present. I am Nadine... I am Hope."

1-13-2017

This is Clara Bullrich, Managing Director of Guggenheim Latin America. She is from Argentina. She currently lives in Miami where she flies from to coach with Steve. Wow!

1-13-17

Lil Eskey and her children Roman and Delaney added to the family wall where "The Tree of Life" will be painted.

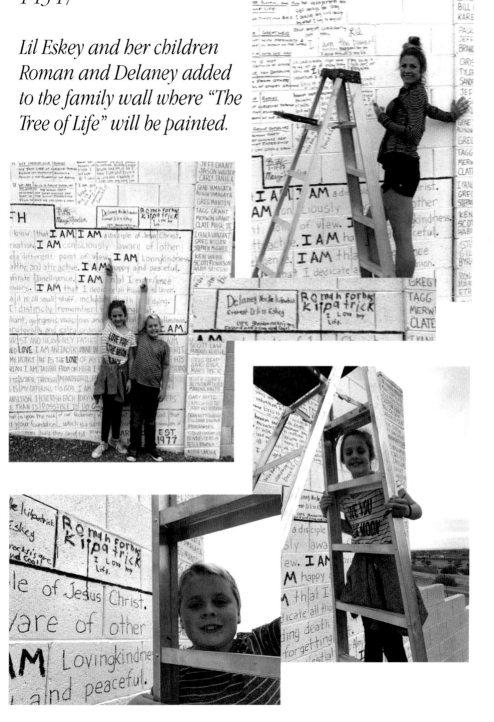

1-13-17

Erik Eskey, Lil's husband adding his declaration to the family wall.

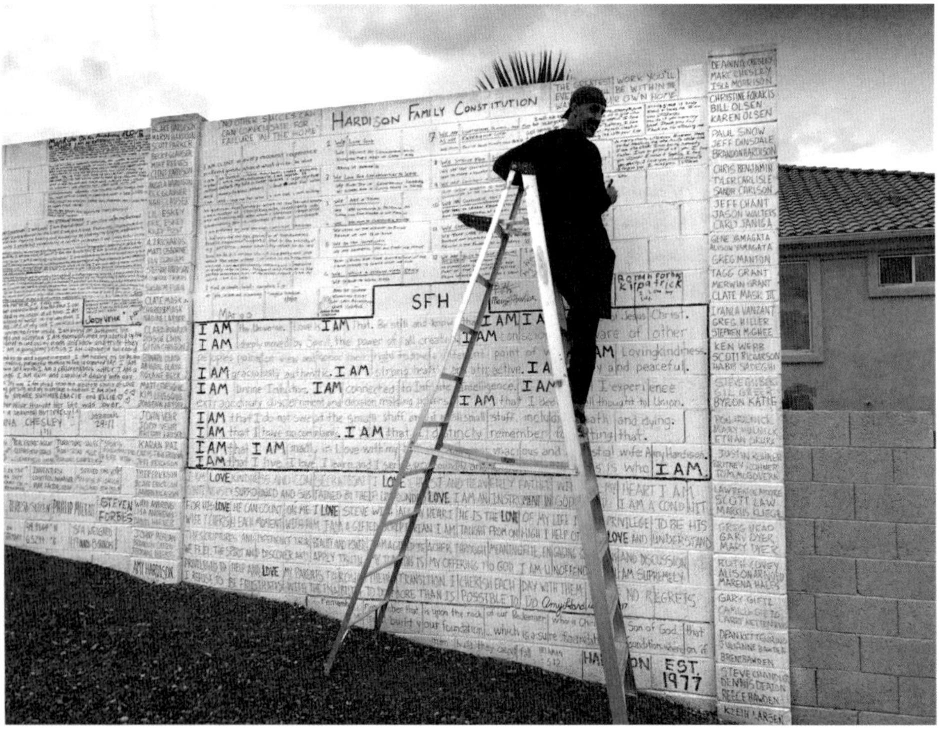

1-14-17

Steffany Hardison went "all in" when she added to the wall. Love what she wrote!

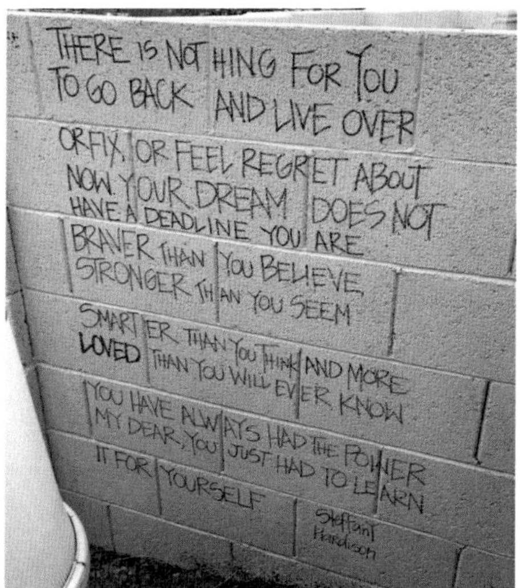

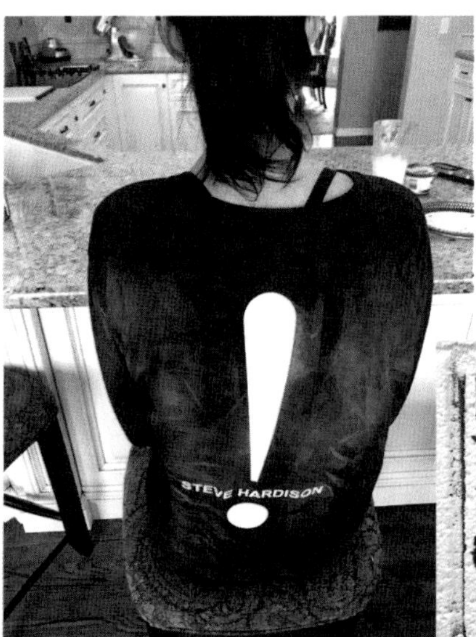

NEVER WATER
YOURSELF DOWN JUST
BECAUSE SOMEONE CAN'T
HANDLE YOU AT 100 PROOF
SH

1-14-2017

More powerful and truthful words added to the wall.

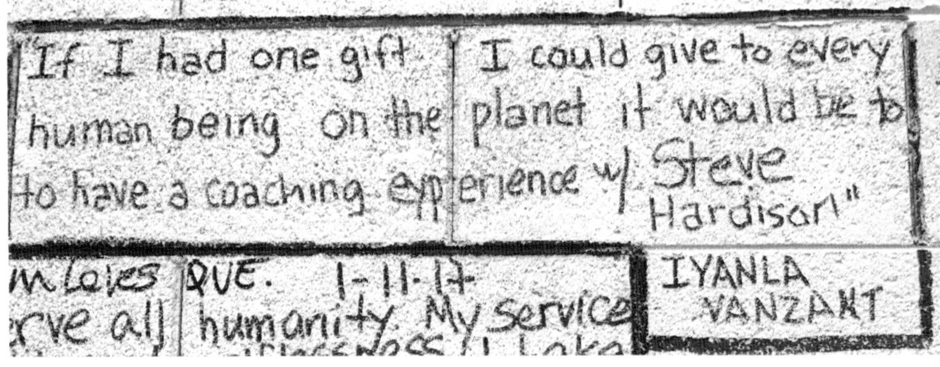

1-14-2017

Dr. Daniel Harner shared his declaration. He drove two hours from Flagstaff to write on The 11:11 Masterpiece canvas.

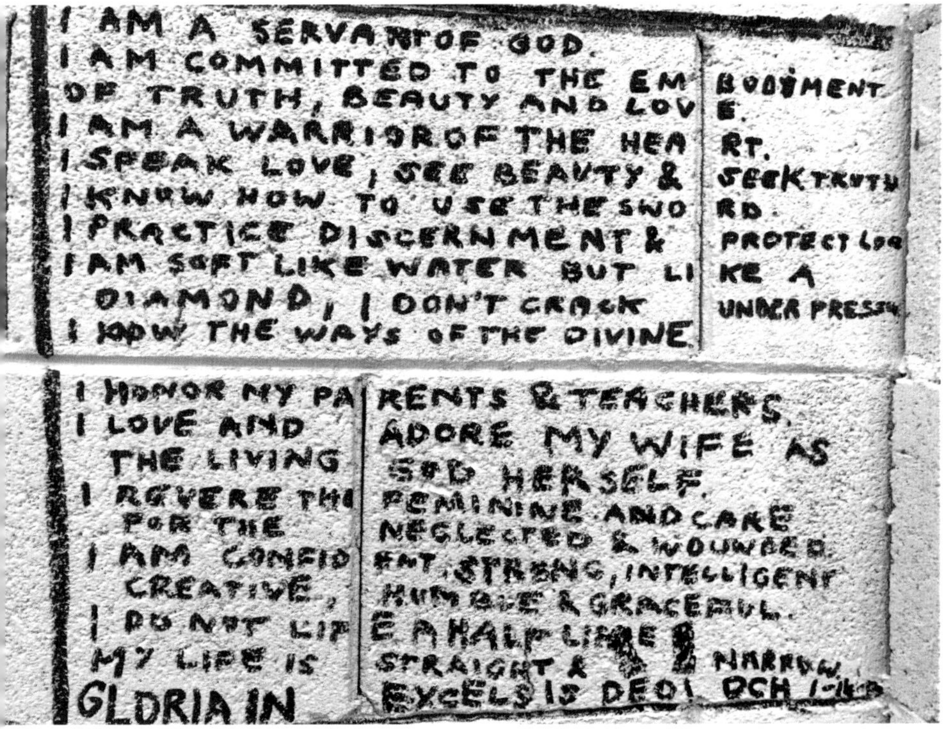

I AM A SERVANT OF GOD.
I AM COMMITTED TO THE EMBODIMENT
OF TRUTH, BEAUTY AND LOVE.
I AM A WARRIOR OF THE HEART.
I SPEAK LOVE, SEE BEAUTY & SEEK TRUTH
I KNOW HOW TO USE THE SWORD.
I PRACTICE DISCERNMENT & PROTECT LOO
I AM SOFT LIKE WATER BUT LIKE A
DIAMOND, I DON'T CRACK UNDER PRESSU
I KNOW THE WAYS OF THE DIVINE.

I HONOR MY PARENTS & TEACHERS.
I LOVE AND ADORE MY WIFE AS
THE LIVING GOD HERSELF.
I REVERE THE FEMININE AND CARE
FOR THE NEGLECTED & WOUNDED.
I AM CONFIDENT, STRONG, INTELLIGENT
CREATIVE, HUMBLE & GRACEFUL.
I DO NOT LIVE A HALF LIFE
MY LIFE IS STRAIGHT & NARROW.
GLORIA IN EXCELSIS DEO! DCH 1-14

1-14-2017

I continue to feel overwhelmed by all that is happening. I receive texts every day with photos attached from Steve. Photos of his clients and family writing their declarations on the wall.

The declarations created by digging deep in to who they are at the core of their being. The "I Am" of "who they be" that's so much more than an "I am" statement.

> *"And God said unto Moses, I AM THAT I AM: And he said Thus shalt thou say unto the children of Israel, I AM hath sent me unto you." Exodus 3:14*

One of the most important things I learned in my time coaching with Steve is that "I am that I am."

The people writing on the wall have created something far more meaningful, magical and miraculous than I could have ever dreamed myself. I had no expectation, but it far exceeds my vision in ways I don't have words to describe.

I learned today that I have permission from every person who wrote on the wall to share publicly what they wrote. What a huge gift to me and every other person who gets to experience their declarations.

The quality of people who shared what they shared on the wall is a true testament to how special Steve is in what he does and creates with people as The Ultimate Coach.

I asked God to send me the best coach there was. The best one on the planet. A week or two later, Steve Hardison walked up to me in a parking garage and introduced himself. It's all incredibly miraculous.

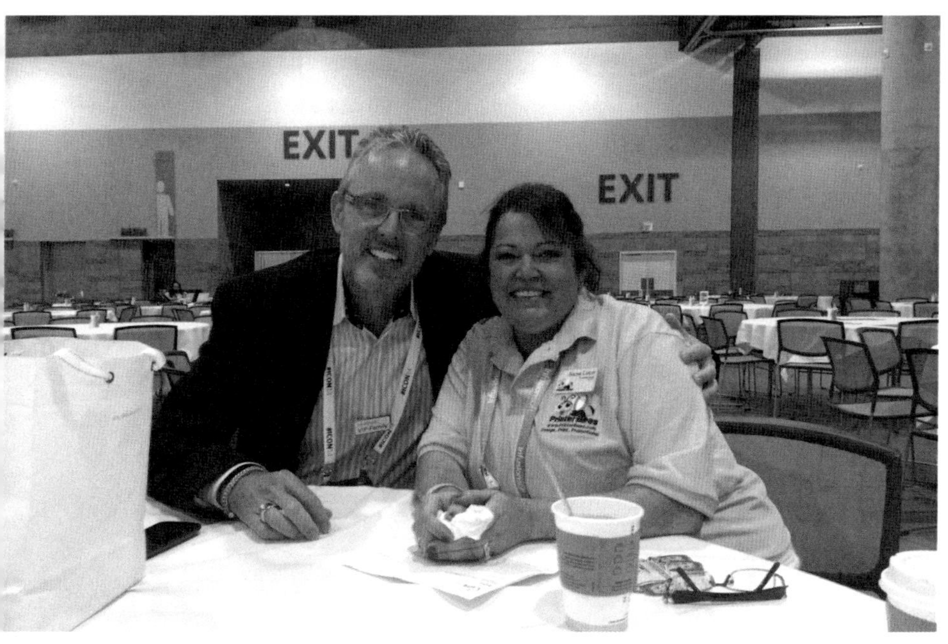

A photo from when I first met Steve on April 23rd, 2014.

1-14-17

I am that I am…

"I am an artist that touches people around the world with my story, my art and my expression. I am the best at what I do, my light shines so bright it's almost blinding, as does my authenticity and my brilliance. I show people the light that is God and I live the greatest expression of the life gifted to me by God. I treasure every moment and I remain present. I am Nadine, I am Hope … I am that I am."

1-15-2017

Incredibly moved to receive family photos from Steve and Amy's family in front of the wall they all signed.

1-16-2017

Lanny D. Owens adding his words on the wall.

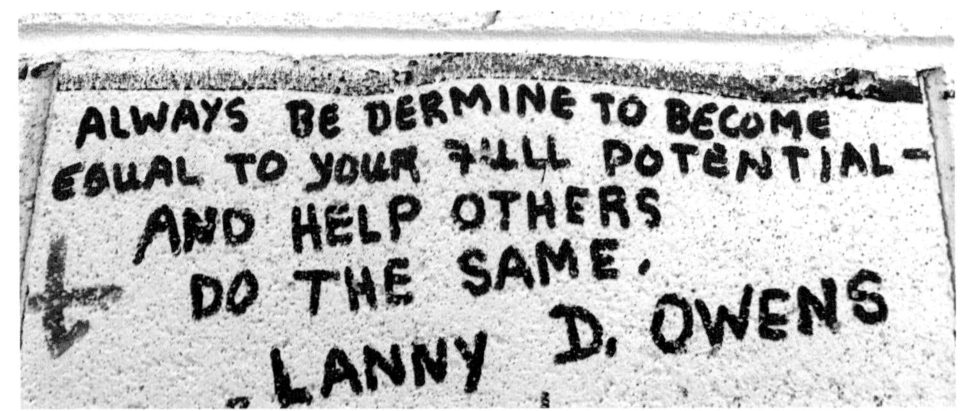

1-17-2017

Christine Erickson, CEO of Erickson Inc.

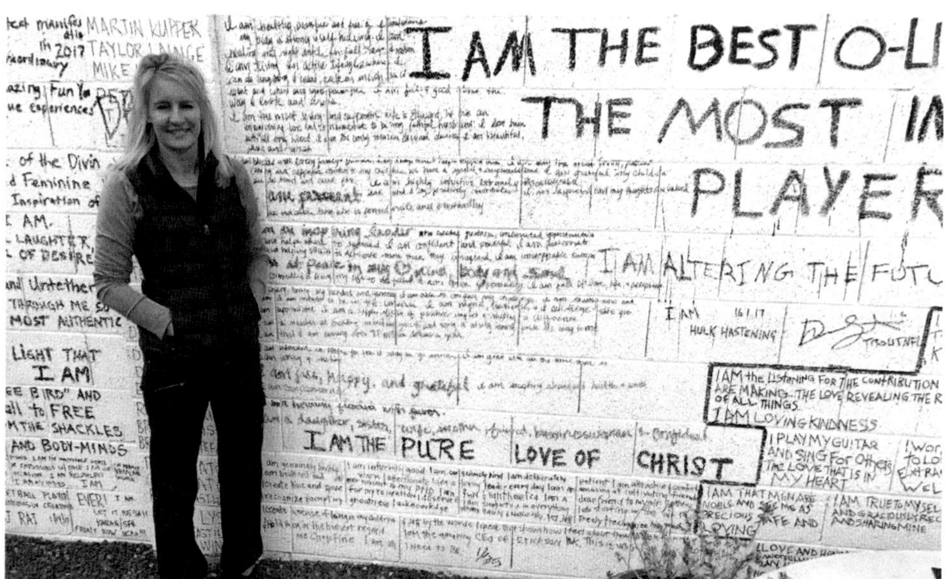

1-17-2017

AJ Richards, creator of Rush Club Nation.

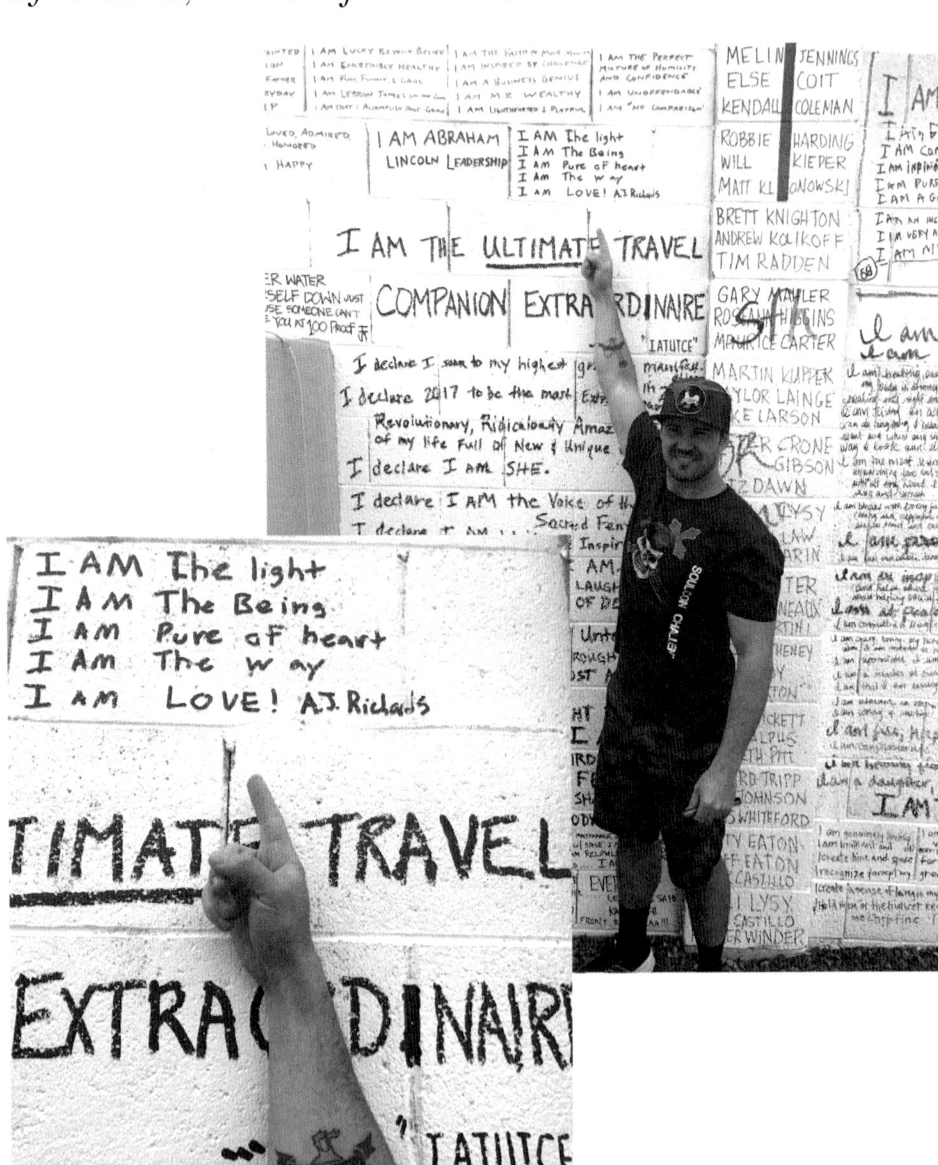

1-17-2017

Edward Olaya, co-owner of Venue at the Grove in Phoenix; father a triplet girls: Ava, Adelina, and Audrey. He is married to Abigail Olaya who also signed the wall and coaches with Steve. He is writing his "My Blueprint" on the wall.

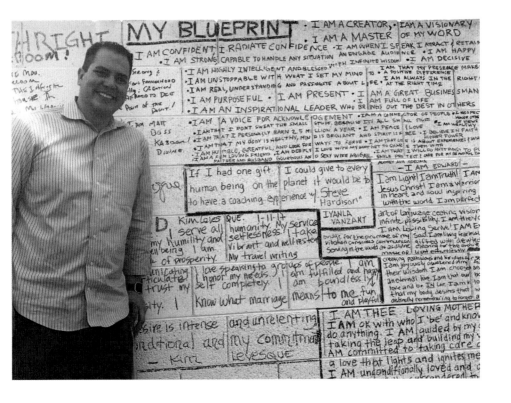

1-17-2017

Today's last photo says "Do not read this sign."

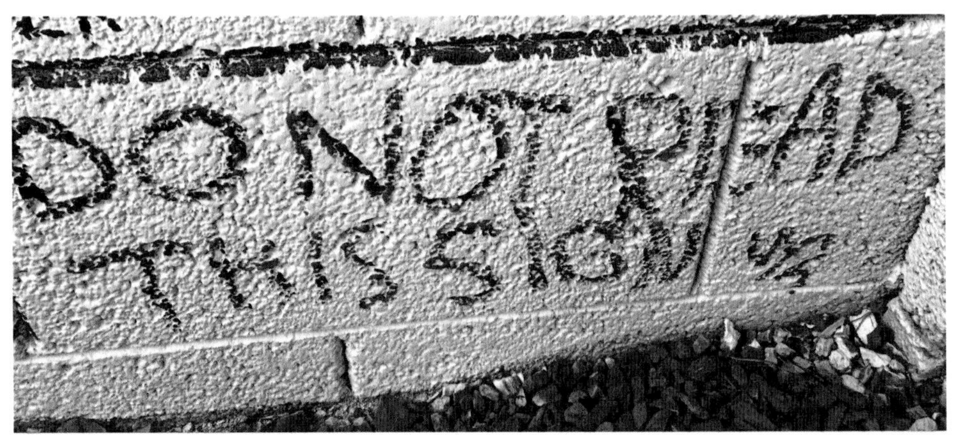

When I asked who added this to the wall…

This was what I received from prankster Steve… He really is so funny and IS a prankster! :-)

Me, I am a prankster, among other things. It is on a block that is difficult to get to or see. I did not want an empty block:)

1-18-2017

Ward Andrews, CEO of Drawbackwards.

1-19-2017

JP Morgan Jr.

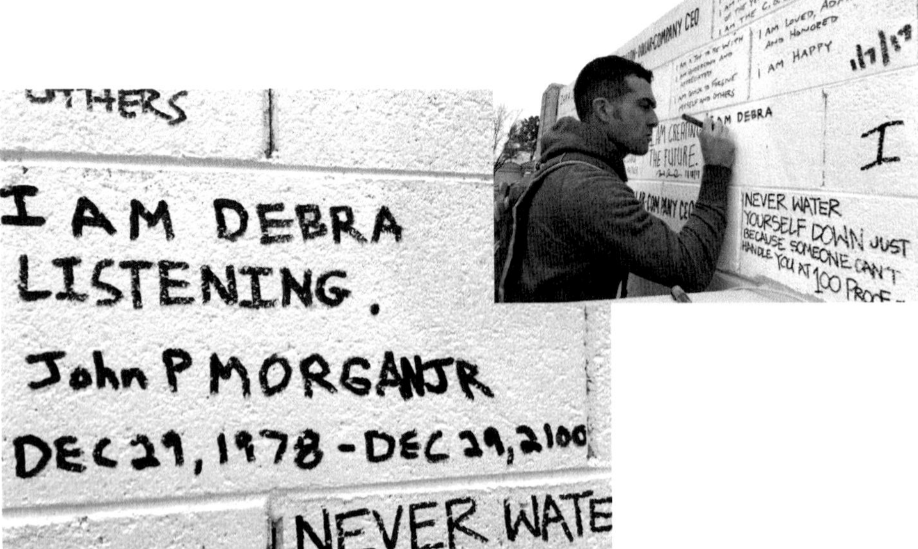

1-19-2017

The wall is almost completely full.

"Feel the Life Force Energy." SFH

Steve worked incredibly hard with his clients and family to have all of this "Life Force Energy" on the wall for me to paint on. The number of hours invested in prepping this wall for my art is not measurable. I'm incredibly grateful for all that has gone in to preparing this wall.

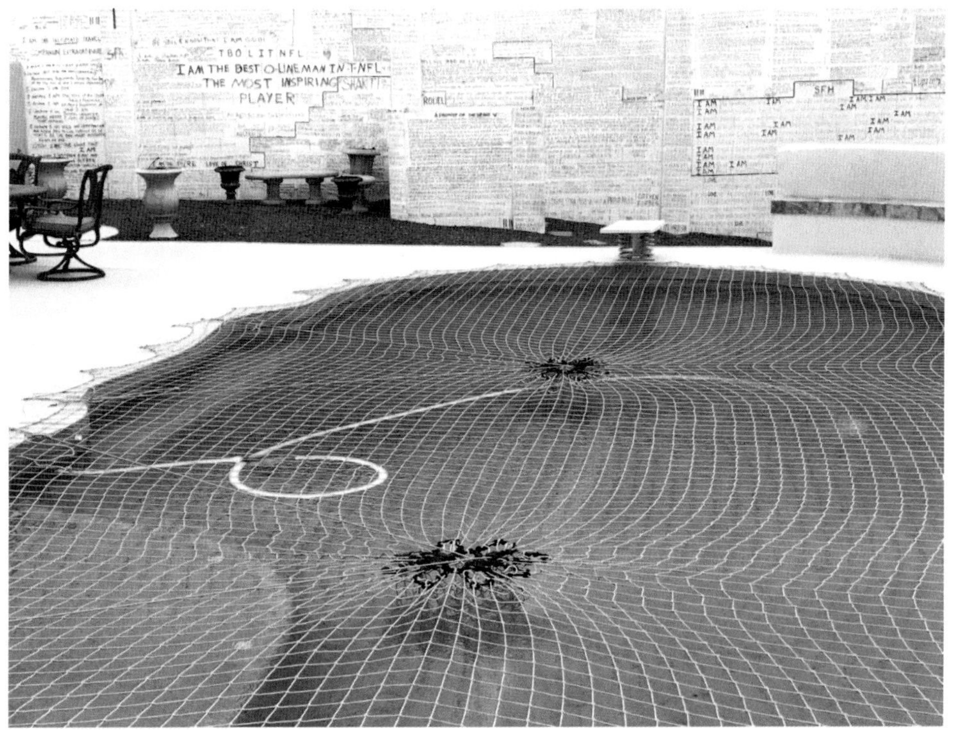

1-20-2017

Josue Lain! This is Josue's "Simpliciti." Rain or shine, nothing can stop the magic happening at The 11:11 Masterpiece Wall.

1-21-2017

Notes from Steve…

"The 11:11 Masterpiece "Canvas" as of 1-21-17 3:11 p.m. Loving you. Be Blessed. SFH"

The Love, The Light, and The Energy of the 11:11 Masterpiece!!

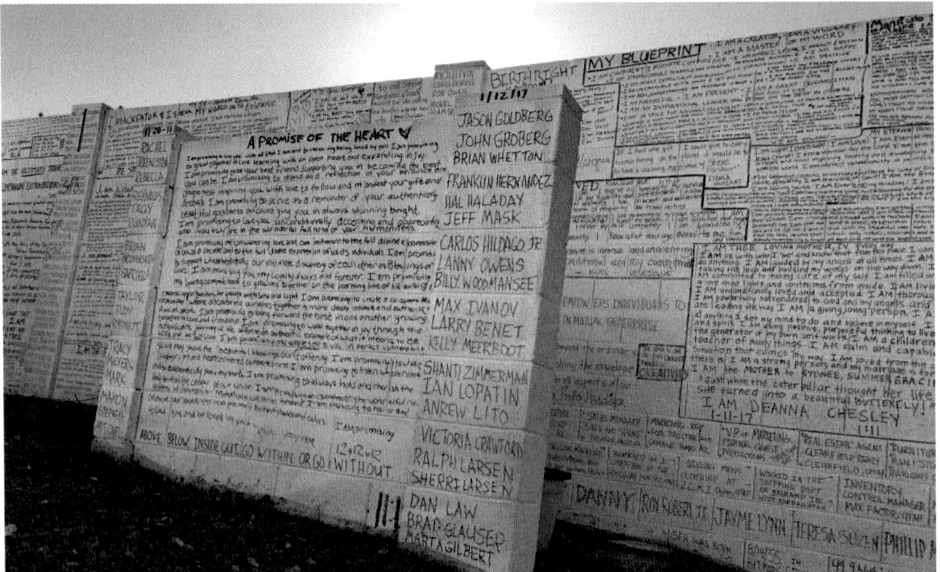

1-22-2017

Nick and Kellie Huntington of Sweetcakes and a key player in the creation of TBOLITNFL came to sign the wall. Nick is a friend of mine on Facebook and has been so kind and supportive. I look forward to meeting these two amazing people in person!

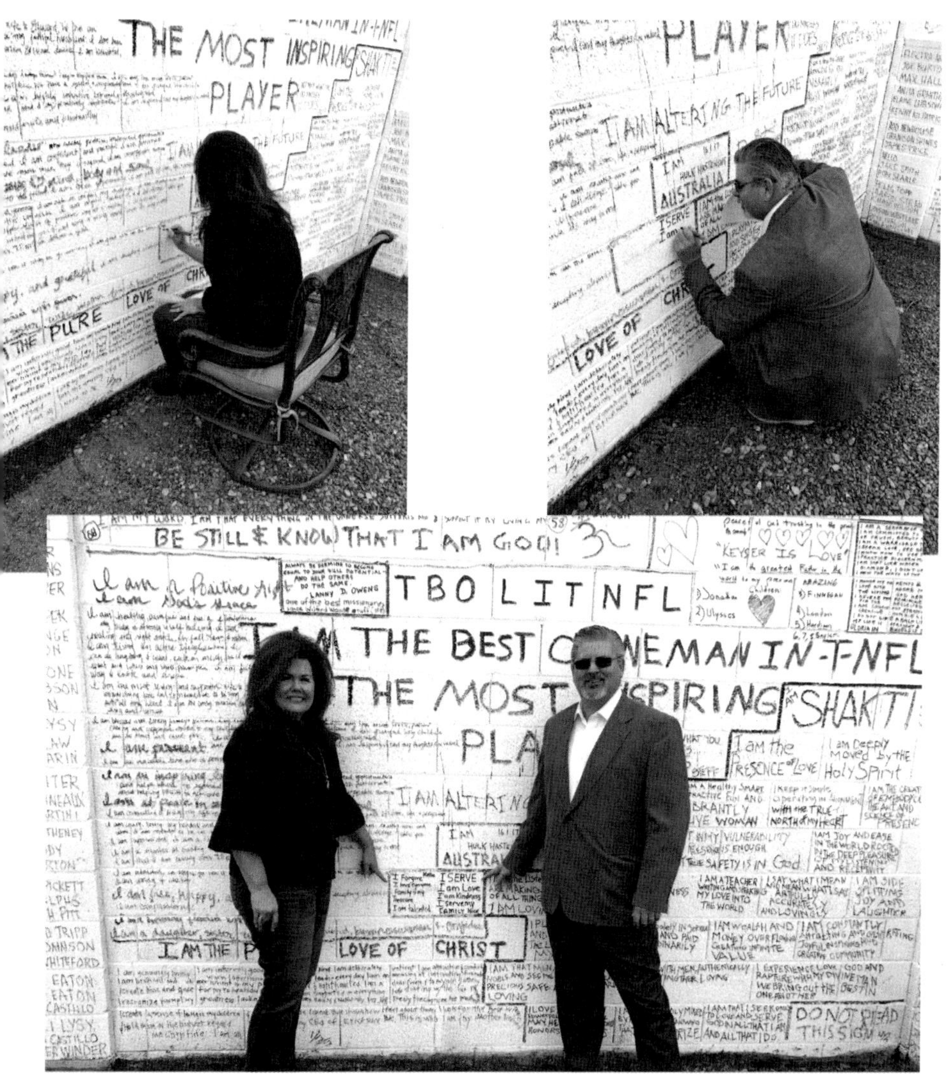

1-22-2017

Steve is looking good in front of the wall! It's almost ready for some art! I am so moved by all of the words and energy on the wall. Absolutely incredible.

1-22-17

"For me: The most Sacred Place on earth. My sanctuary just southwest of the 11:11 Masterpiece." SFH

1-24-2017

Jeff Erickson, dentist and creator of the NSFC of Arizona.

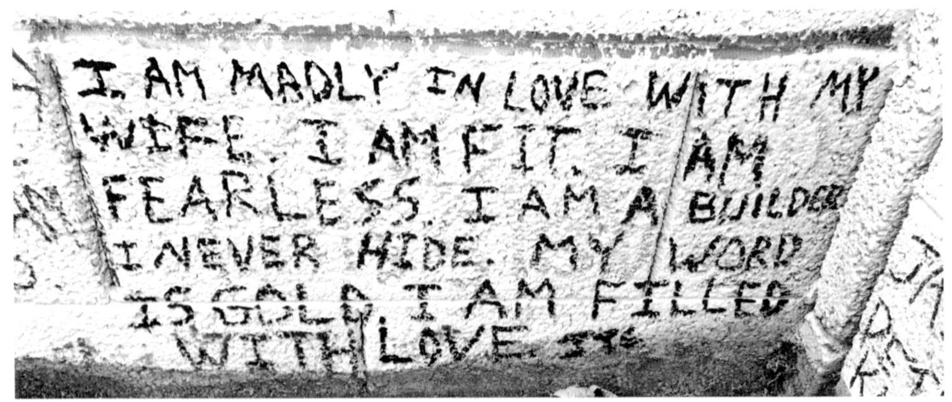

1-24-2017

Greg Head stopped by to write on the wall while Steve was with a client.

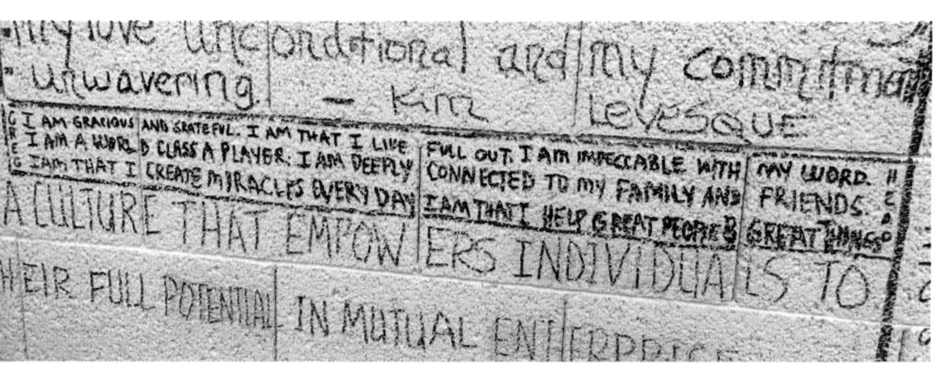

1-29-2017

Being sick in bed when the wall was finally ready for me left me unable to begin painting, which was incredibly frustrating after waiting, watching and experiencing the magic being created at The 11:11 Masterpiece Wall.

I did get this beautiful message from Steve.

This may be the last thing written on the 11:11 Masterpiece. It is part of a blessing I received from a Patriarch by the name of Melvin Wood. It was given to me by the laying on of hands when I was 18 years old on Dec. 4th 1973. I have seen this blessing fulfilled many times in my life. I thank God for the gifts He has given me. Loving you. Be Blessed. SFH

Steve, Dec 4 1973
..."if you keep yourself clean and free from the sins of this
world, many shall be influenced by your life; they will turn to
you for advice, and seeing your good works will follow in
your footsteps and will praise your name forever, as well as
being honored by your God, who lives and dwells in yonder
heavens."
Your Father (in Heaven)

My response:

Beautiful! Perfect! Not to mention true... I've seen this happen in my own life as a result of knowing/watching you. ❤❤❤

I hope to be there tomorrow to see it in person!!! Paint brush... or paint roller in hand! 🙏

1-29-2017

Oh how I love this amazing man!!! Caring and funny!

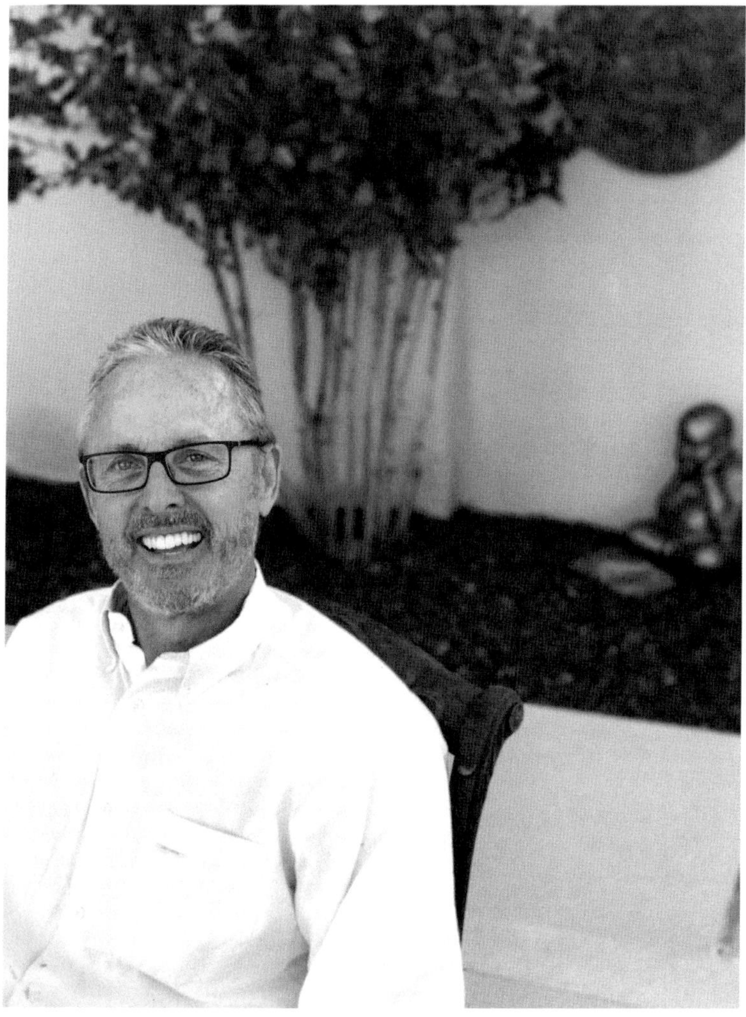

Do not come if you are still not feeling well. Take care of yourself. This wall is not going anywhere:) Loving you. SFH and Buddha:)

1-30-2017

Jermaine Alberts from Australia who comes every other week to meet with Steve found one brick that didn't have writing on it to add his energy to the wall.

I'm blown away by his commitment to come to Phoenix every other week to meet with Steve because Steve only coaches in person. Says a lot about Steve and Jermaine.

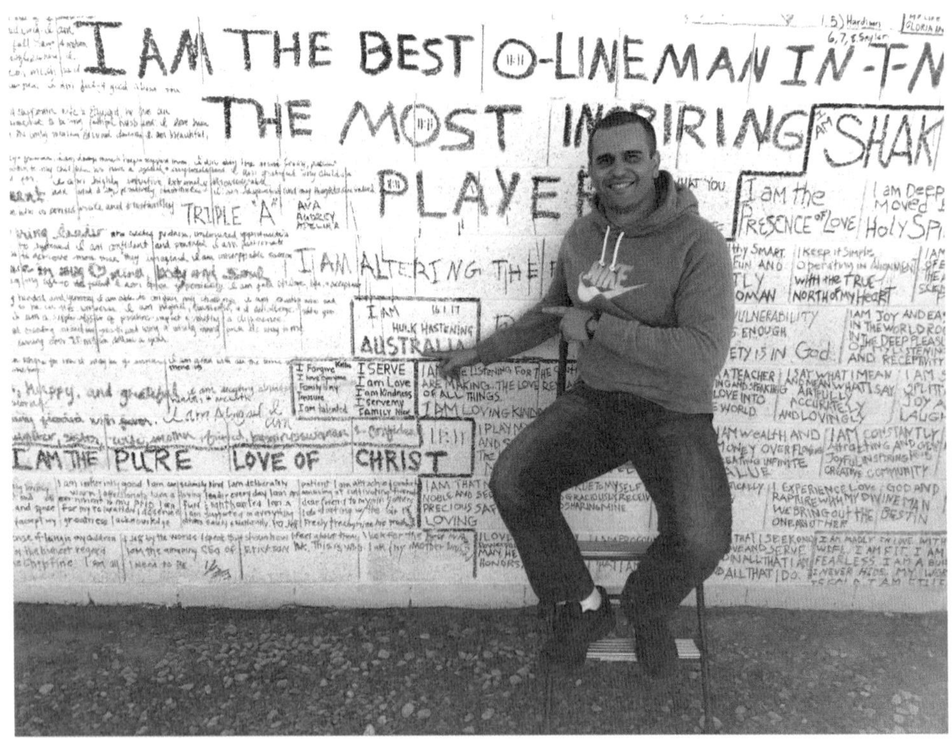

2-2-2017

I was absolutely scared and anxious to begin adding paint. So nervous that I couldn't eat and I thought I may actually vomit at any moment. So scared!!!!

So glad to have my mother in town to help me get started. She was a great support and so encouraging to me. What a blessing! Made a huge difference in my ability to start.

I was also blessed to have Jody Vehr present to encourage me on this journey. Steve is amazing in every way! I have tremendous gratitude.

What an amazing day to get started!

2-2-2017

Let the painting begin!!!! I did it!!! I got the paint on the wall and am on my way to creating this "Masterpiece!"

2-6-2017

Karan Rai - A new company was born today in Steve's office! Asgard Partners & Co. An amazing journey shared with amazing people. Loved meeting Karan… what a beautiful soul.

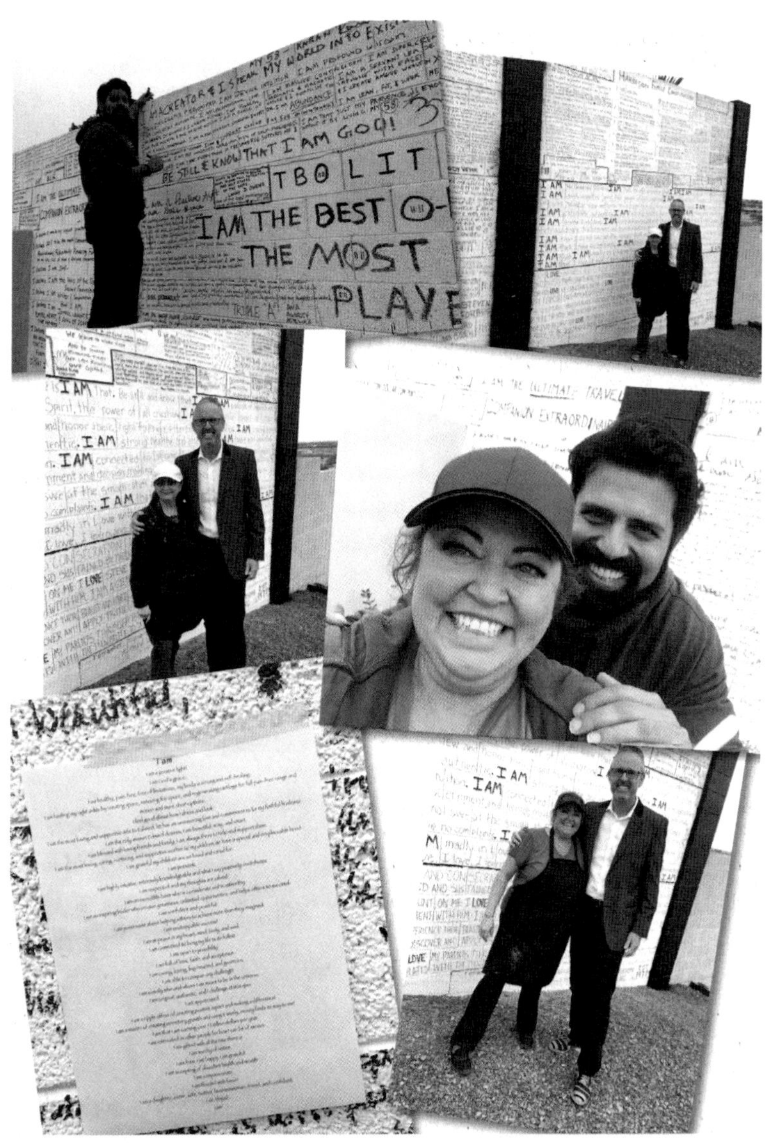

2-6-2017

"Go Within or Go Without" is well under way, my fear and angst is subsiding. Thank God! Feeling so much better.

2-7-2017

Mom and I went in the evening so I could use a projector to trace the outlines of the images I plan to add to the canvas/ wall. Mom was a huge help! The sunset was beautiful and amazing.

2-8-2017

Love what Steve wrote on this wall! I cried as I read it. I enjoyed meeting Ward Andrews as he added his declarations to The 11:11 Masterpiece Wall.

2-9-2017

Continued progress on "Go Within or Go Without." Feeling proud at how it's coming along as it nears completion.

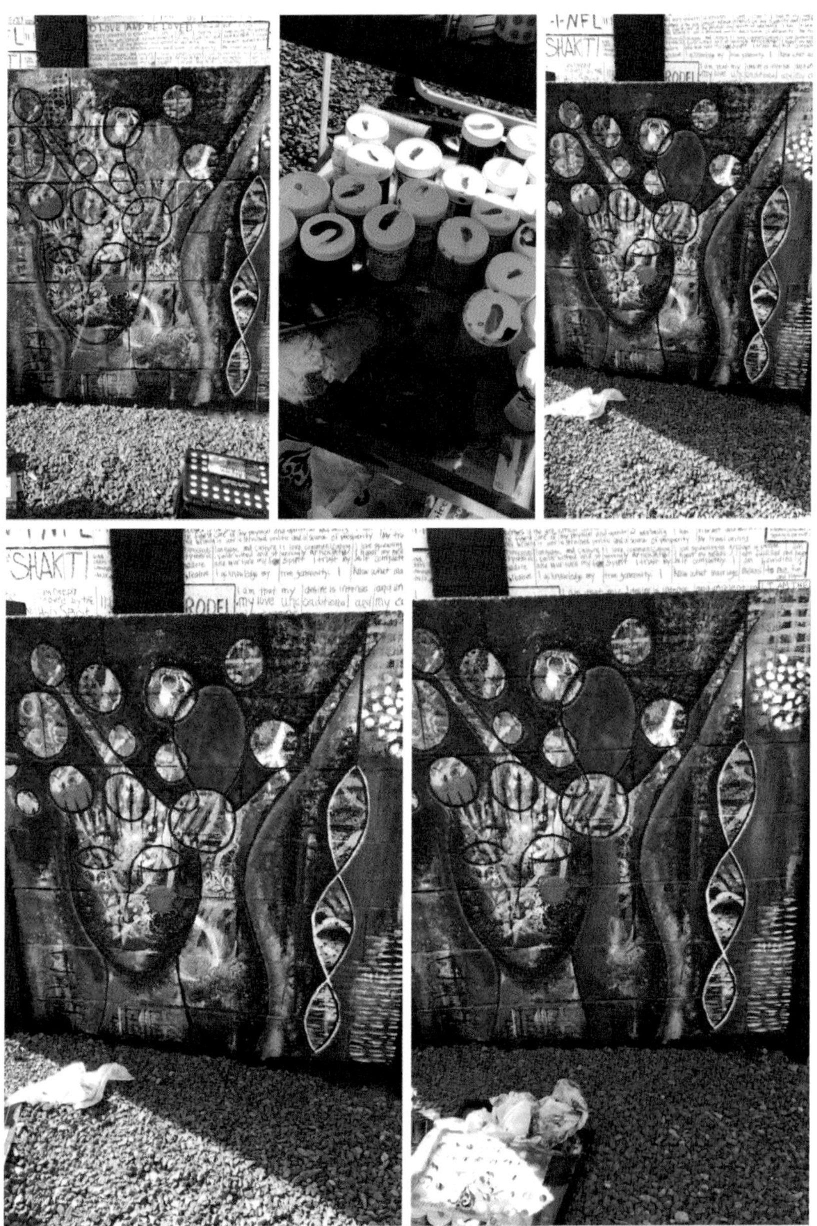

2-13-2017

Text messages from Steve along the way never get old. How can I fail with this amount of support? Blows my mind.

Nadine Larder aka "My Picasso".

A Master in Action completing Go Within or Go Without.

You are a Master. I am so pleased with the result!!! Loving you are your impeccable work. Thank you for putting your life force, your passion, and your excellence into the wall know as the 11:11 Masterpiece by Nadine Larder. I honor, respect, and admire your gifts. You are my Picasso. SFH

2-13-2017

So blessed to meet Dr. Roxane Beck and Jermaine Alberts today. Jermaine flies from Australia and Roxane flies in from Florida. That's commitment!

2-13-2017

"Go Within or Go Without" is complete!!!! Feeling so proud of myself. Steve and Amy loved it too. Celebration time!

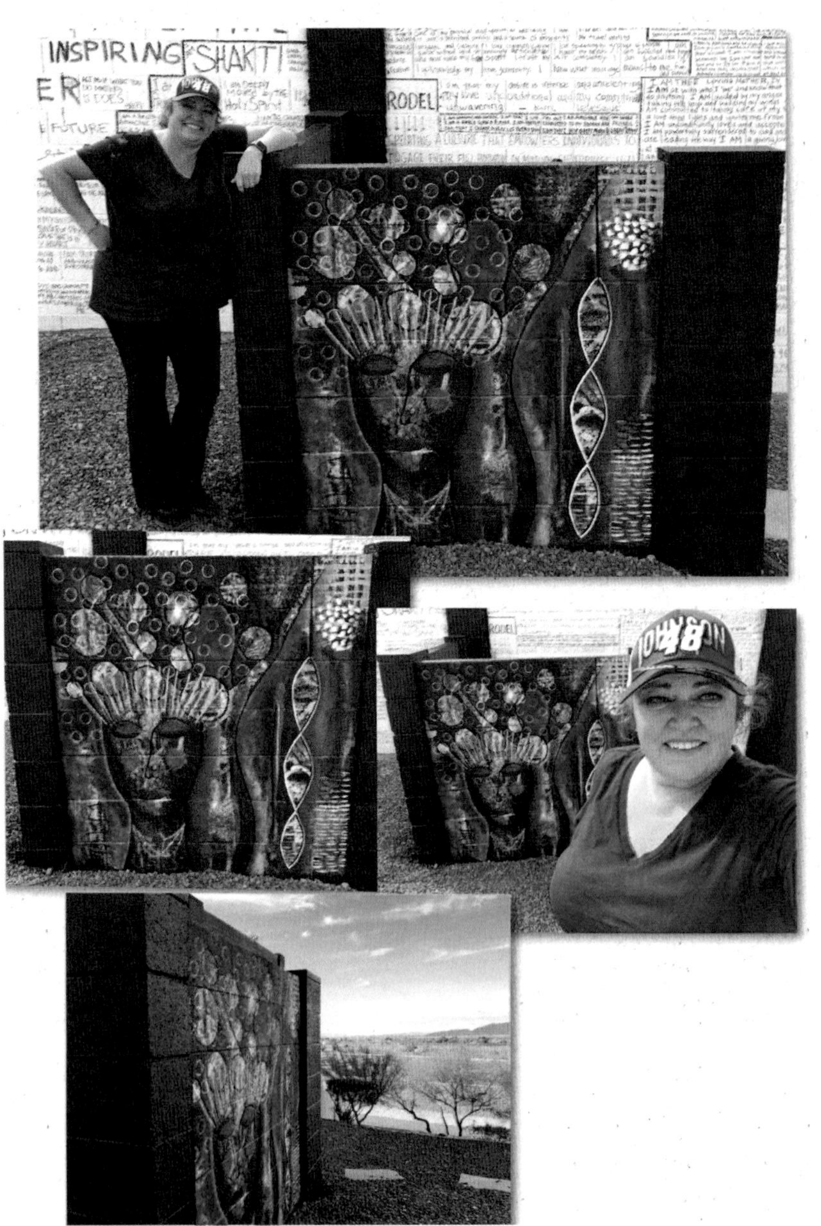

2-14-2017

Tom came out to help me put a base layer of paint down for "The Tree of Life." I'm nervous to get started, but holding on to faith that I can do this! So thankful to have Tom's help on this.

2-15-2017

The scaffolding is up and it's time to begin painting and creating this 13 ft. tall "Tree of Life." Fighting through the fear and carrying on. I've got this!!!

I've had so much fun with Steve in the creation of The 11:11 Masterpiece Wall. Today I invited him to come on up… and he did! Steve standing in front of the scaffolding shows how tall it is. Steve is 6' 4". That wall is huge!

2-16-2017

I'm making progress on this huge tree. Still fighting through my doubts and fears of my ability to paint this tree. My nerves are a bit of a wreck... but "I've got this!"

2-21-2017

My tree is making tremendous progress. OH My Gosh! It's coming together. Steve sent a photo of what it looks like at night!

2-21-2017

What a treat for me today. Steve made me one of his famous PB & J sandwiches for lunch! I decided to stay late to meet up with Elizabeth Pitt, who was coming to see Steve and the wall. Lunch with Steve was as you would expect. Awesome! Wisdom filled and great conversation. It was great to meet Elizabeth! We identified the exact brick her name is on behind the paint.

My "fashion" while painting is quite interesting… I mean totally embarrassing. What's a girl who's painting a wall to do?

2-22-2017

Steve helping me work through my own doubts, which seem to be center stage at the moment. Powerful words to live by. I'm making great progress !

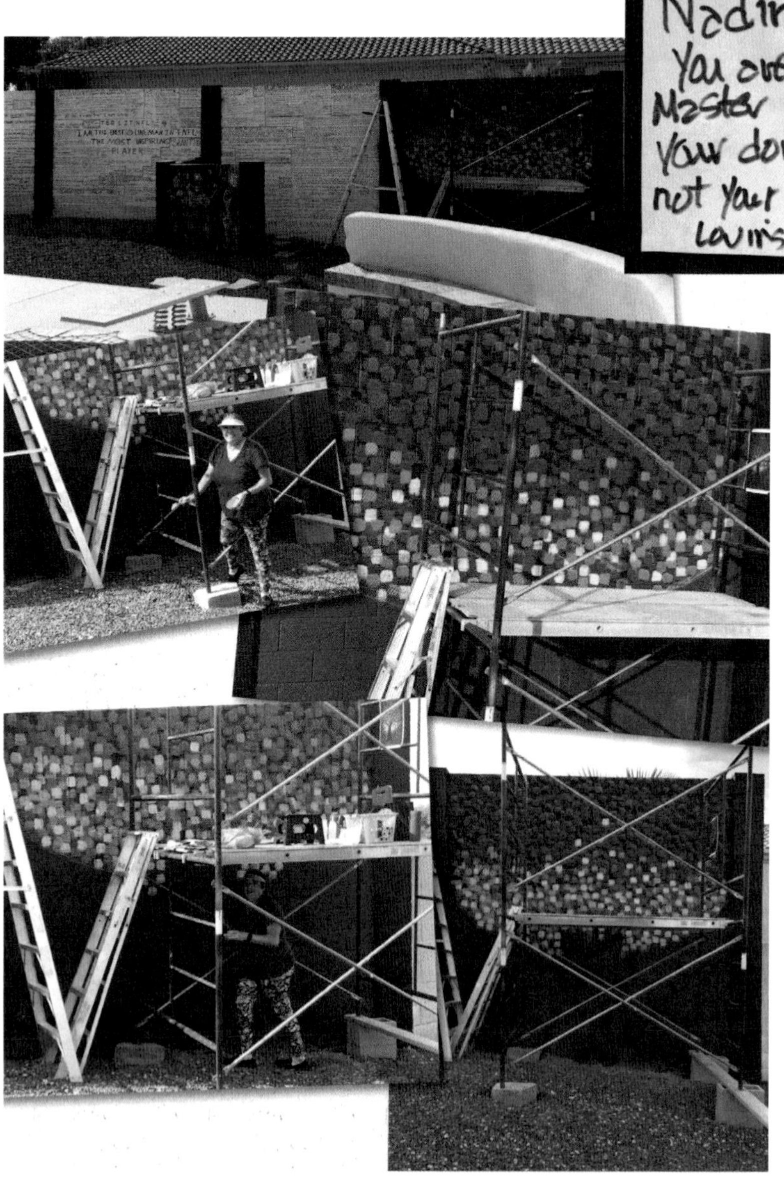

2-23-2017

Early morning photos from Steve to show my tree in the morning sunshine. OMGosh!!! It's so beautiful.

I can't believe I painted that!!! Thousands of brush strokes, one brush stroke at a time.

2-23-2017

Steve is good at sneaking up on me while I'm working away to take photos. It makes it all the more fun to be there. Never a dull moment, which I thoroughly enjoy.

2-27-2017

I wasn't able to paint today and won't be able to paint tomorrow either due to rain.

I was making such great progress and it's disappointing to not be able to "get back to my tree."

I worked through my doubts with some support and encouragement from Steve and Amy. I can't wait to complete this tree that has such meaning to both of them.

What they both shared with me from The Book of Mormon (Nephi Chapter 8:1) really brought home the meaning of "The Tree of Life" for them. It's a story called "Lehi's dream" and it's beautiful.

"The Tree of Life" will be beautiful when it's done!

3-1-2017

One of the gifts in creating this mural is the people I get to meet as they come from coaching. Jonathan Keyser is awesome! And my tree is looking amazing!

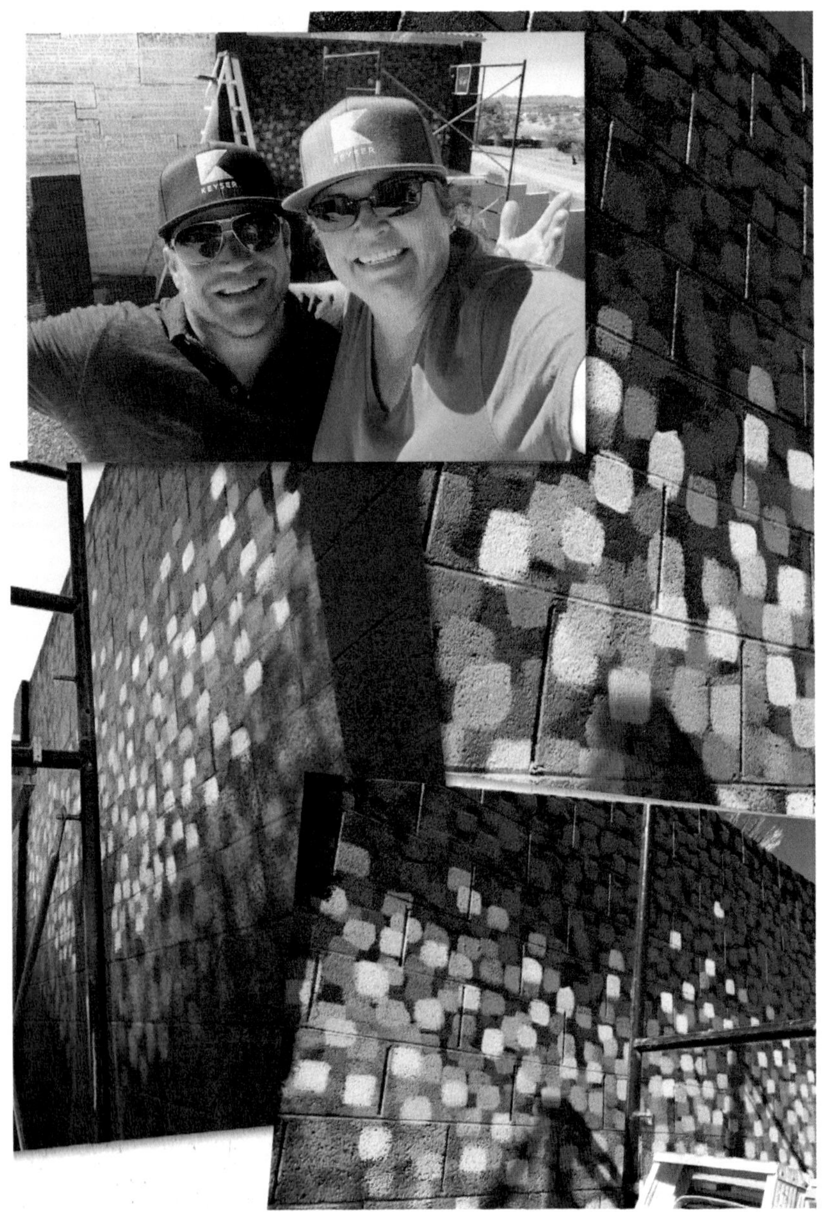

3-2-2017

"The Tree of Life" continues to come alive. I love how it looks, I'm feeling really proud of myself.

3-3-2017

I have touched this wall with a paint brush thousands of times. I feel so proud of how it's coming together and I can't wait to get the scaffolding moved so I can see it better.

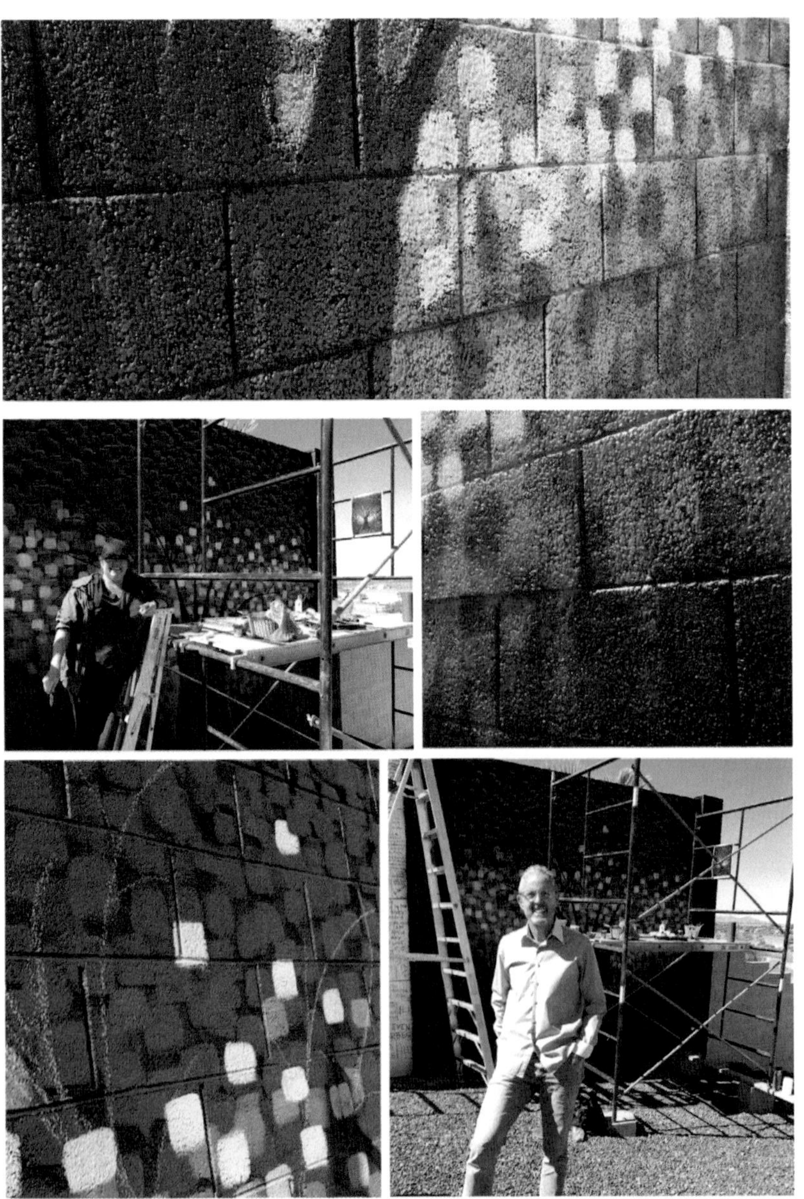

3-3-2017

When I was able to see "The Tree of Life" with the scaffolding removed, I cried.

3-3-2017

I finished!

"I could not be more pleased with the outcome of "The Tree of Life." SFH

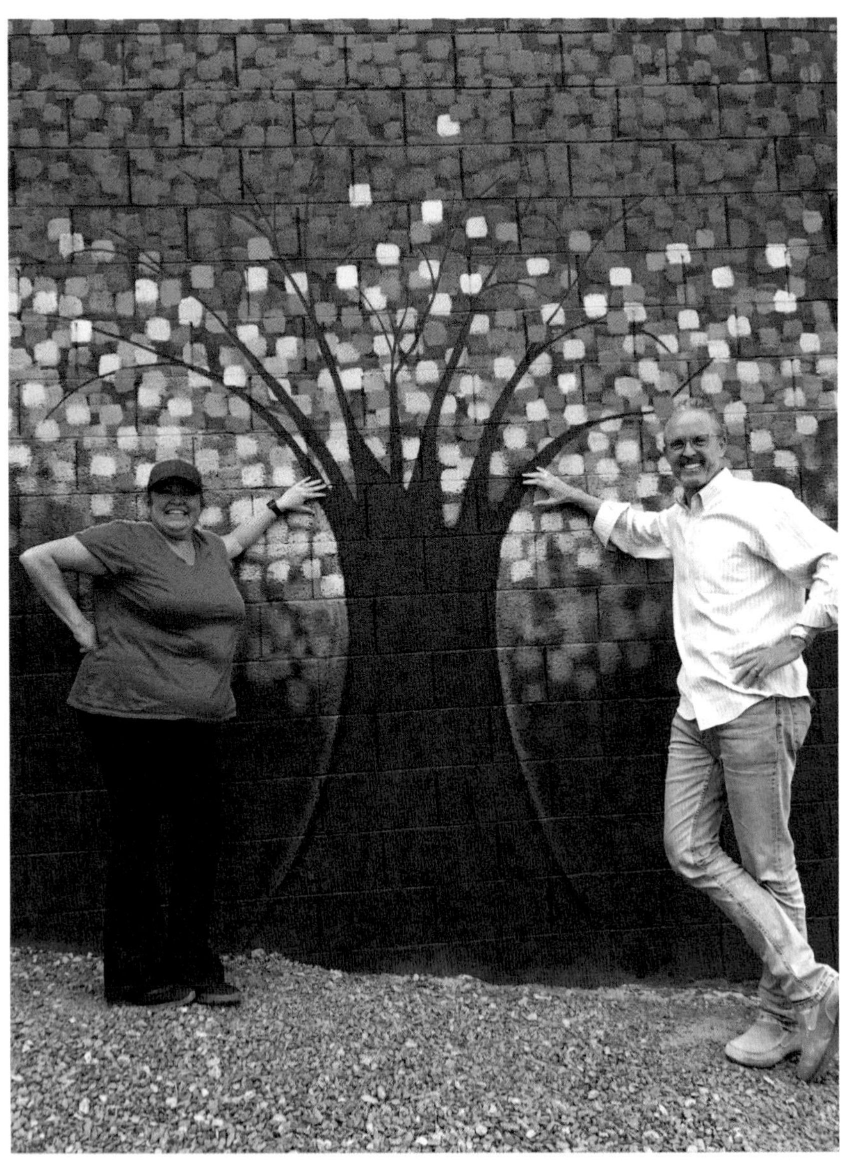

3-3-2017

I love when I have the opportunity to see Amy and visit with her. It's been such a treat to get to know her while I'm here working on the wall. She's a beautiful soul. I love her. She loves the tree.

3-3-2017

Today was an absolute treat to meet Dr. Daniel Harner. He gifted me with his presence and a beautiful poem.

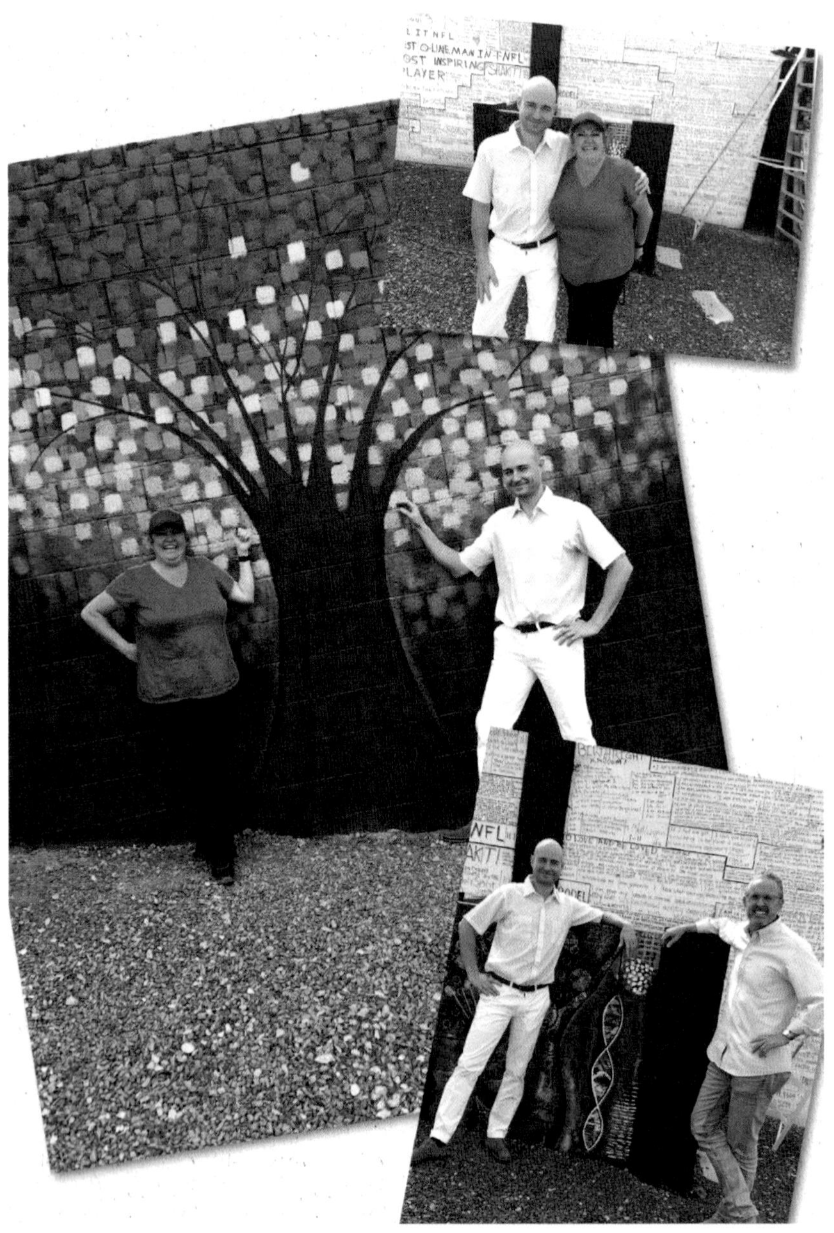

3-4-2017

Steve let me know he got a new pet today. Her home will be next to The 11:11 Masterpiece Wall, she is eleven years old, so her name is Eleven.

3-6-2017

Today brought the beginning of a new canvas, "No Mud, No Lotus, The 1000 Petal Lotus."

I found myself in a space of fear and doubt again… not knowing where to begin as I stared at the wall… staring back at me. It invited me to paint with all of the beauty of the words and wisdom on it.

After procrastinating, I finally started adding paint. Looking forward to the journey as I power through my own doubts, insecurities and limited thinking.

3-6-2017

Abigail Olaya said she was really looking forward to seeing the tree in person. I enjoyed seeing her and having a photo op! I never tire of meeting Steve's amazing clients, the people who graciously shared a piece of themselves on the wall I'm painting.

3-6-2017

It's always a treat to see Karan Rai! He's been so supportive.

3-7-2017

Added a second layer of paint to the lotus flower wall. I enjoy this part of the intuitive process while playing with paint. Following the paint and the colors where they want to take me.

3-7-2017

Meeting and spending time with Gina "Shakti" Carlson was a huge treat. She has an amazing energy and spirit. Special day… Special people.

3-7-2017

Jeff Erickson was so kind to take a photo. Steve enjoyed sneaking up on me to take photos while I work. Fun! Fun! Fun!

3-8-2017

Steve accepted my invitation to add paint to the wall with his "ratfink" image. I'm making amazing progress.

3-9-2017

Today brought John Vehr to add paint to the wall. So fun to have people add their art and marks to my wall. I LOVE it! I love when I get to see John when he comes for coaching, he gives the most amazing hugs ever!

3-9-2017

Lessons from the wall…

I'm struggling with my body issues as a result of all the photos. What I dislike about myself, staring me right in the face. Making me face myself. Challenging me to accept myself.

Would I prefer not to be part of the photos and the documentation of what I'm creating? Hell NO! Listen to how ridiculous it sounds. "Don't take my picture while I'm creating my art, I don't like the way I look, I have paint on my clothes and feel too fluffy."

I'm literally picking on myself! How can I thrive to be all I'm capable of when I'm the one picking on me?

People who like me, my art or both don't like me less because of the size of my waist. It's me that's not accepting me because of the size of my waist. I'm the one judging me!

Add to all the judgement and self loathing the impact on my physical well-being. Why would I take extra good care of something I don't like? Ponder that!!! People don't take precious care of things they don't like. I'm not currently taking extra good care of my physical well-being.

I take excellent care of my spiritual well-being, my creativity and my mind because those are my favorite parts of myself. Again… Ponder that!

Now I need to figure out to change my thinking and mindset around my body image so I can love and care for myself in that regard too!

To Be Continued….

3-10-2017

Steve added literally 1000 petals to the lotus. 1000 petals of light.

3-13-2017

Roxane Beck purchased the canvas of "Powerhouse!" So excited.

I continue to make great progress on "No Mud, No Lotus."

3-14-2017

Getting close to completing "No Mud, No Lotus."

3-15-2017

It was very exciting to have the scaffolding taken down so the entire lotus can be seen. Steve helped me take it down. Team work!

3-15-2017

"No Mud, No Lotus" is complete! I love it!

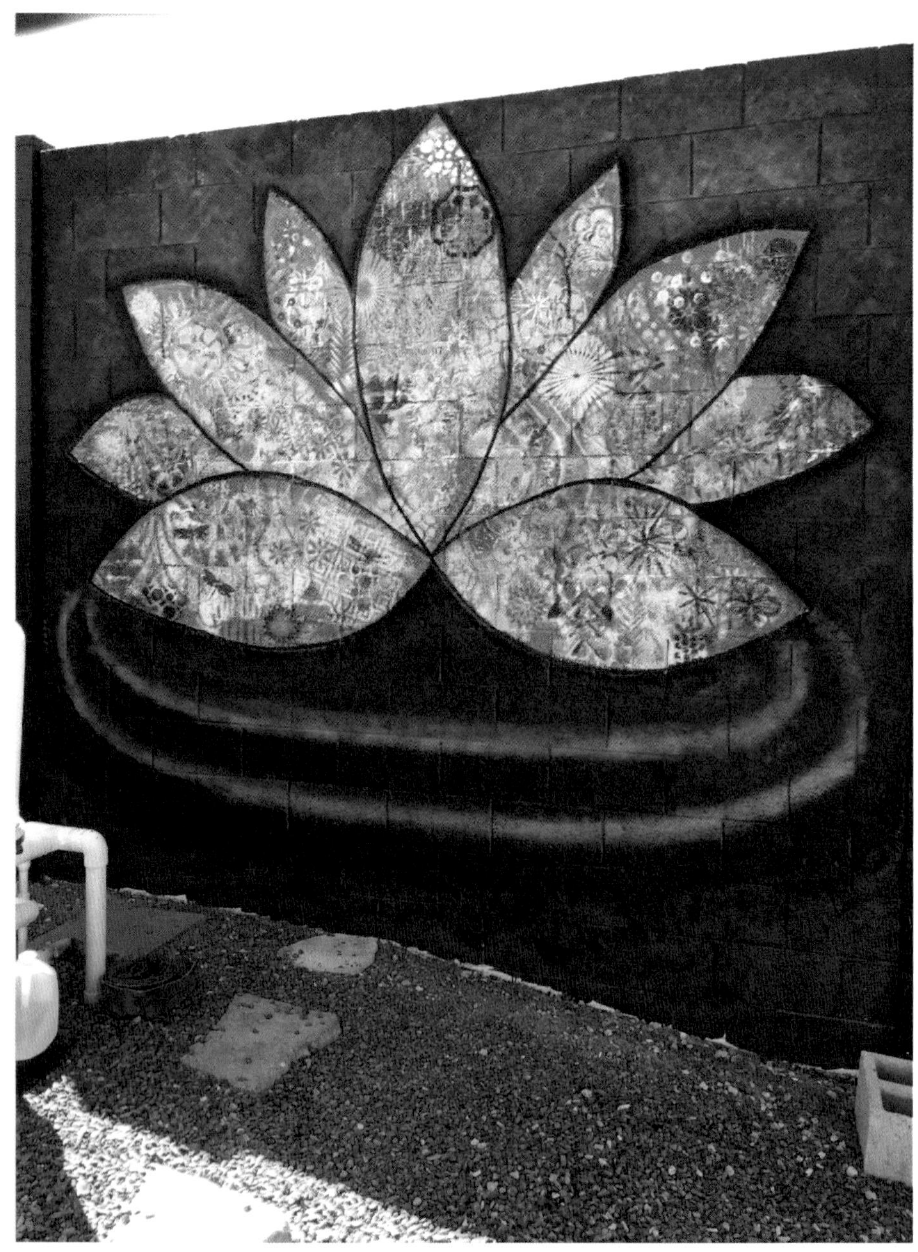

3-20-2017

"The Matriarch" is under way!! "Big Red" added to the wall honoring Steve's mom Maurine Forbes Hardison.

3-21-2017

4-23-14, the day I met Steve Hardison in a parking garage. A life changing day and I knew it when we met. Added to the wall by Steve before I arrived to paint. I was so touched.

3-22-2017

"The Matriarch" is taking shape. The fun never ends too! Jonathan Keyser standing by while I added his logo to the wall. The fact that I can't reach the gate latch is always humorous to 6'4" tall Steve. My paint roller is my "key" to unlatch the gate. 1955 is Steve's birth year.

The music notes on the elephant's ear match the way I say "Hello..." when I broadcast from the wall on Facebook Live.

3-22-2017

Eleven is always around keeping me company. She's awesome! Yes! Steve does walk his turtle. She loves to go to the park to eat dandelions. I added a doodle to the ear of "The Matriarch" in honor of Eleven.

3-23-2017

To say I love how this is evolving is an understatement. I love it!!! Jody Vehr next to "No Mud, No Lotus," where her "Eternal Pryer" is written below the surface. Love her!!! My favorite photo so far of Steve in front of his mural. LOVE! LOVE! LOVE!

3-27-2017

Today I added marks and images that the people who join me for International Paint Party on Facebook Live requested. This is a small sampling of the some of the marks I added for them. I love having the energy of my friends who are walking along side me on this journey, encouraging me from Facebook Live where I share my progress. Had I not had all these amazing people encouraging me and cheering me on, on Facebook over the last two years, this may not have ever happened.

The kindness and encouragement I receive from those who have been painting with me on Facebook Live means everything to me on this journey.

Tremendous Gratitude!

11:11

3-27-2017

"The Matriarch" in progress in the morning sun… glistens!

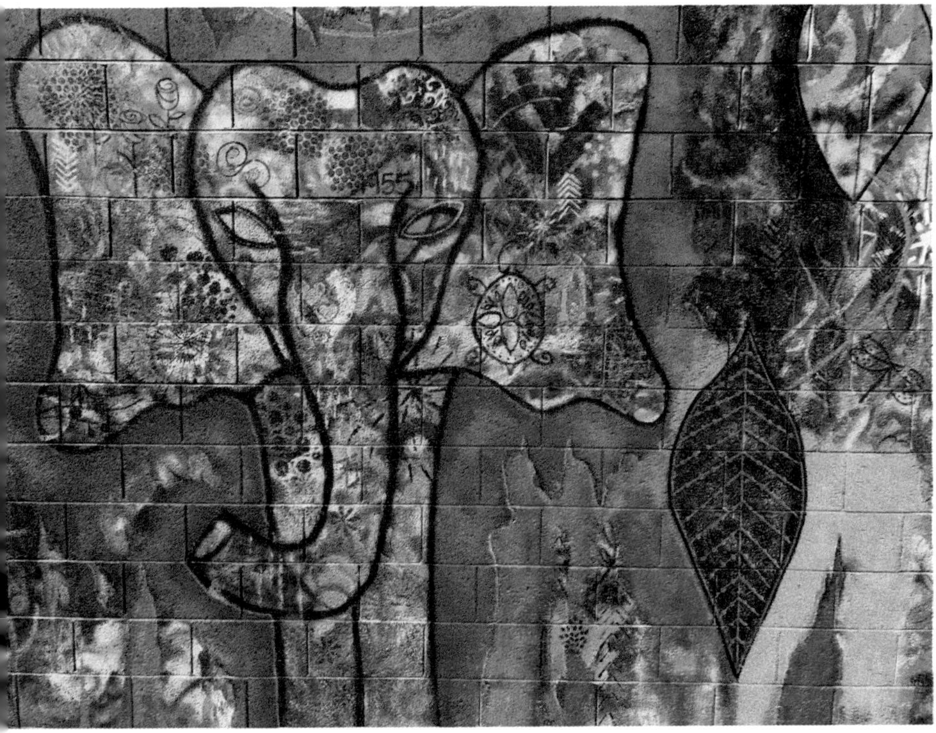

1:8
2 Thess. 5:18
In All things
Give Thanks

3-28-2017

Caught in the act! Painting… Painting… Painting.

3-29-2017

Adding the final touches to "The Matriarch!" I love her!

3-29-2017

"The Matriarch!!!!"

3-29-2017

I couldn't have a better partner in this co-creation! I loved Steve before I started this project and I love him even more after hanging out with him for the last several weeks. He's an incredible human being. What a blessing... I feel tremendously blessed to be here working and creating with Steve.

3-31-2017

I was thrilled to learn that Deanna Chesley was able to stop by and see the completed wall she wrote on … "No Mud, No Lotus."

4-3-2017

Two viking warriors! Ragnar (Karan) and Sebrof (Steve) with "The Matriarch." Sebrof is pointing at the powerful works Ragnar wrote before it was covered.

-2-2017

oday I began the next wall. "Phoenix Rising" is under way. reat to see Abigail who is now the owner of one of my aintings. A gift from Steve and I for her triplets.

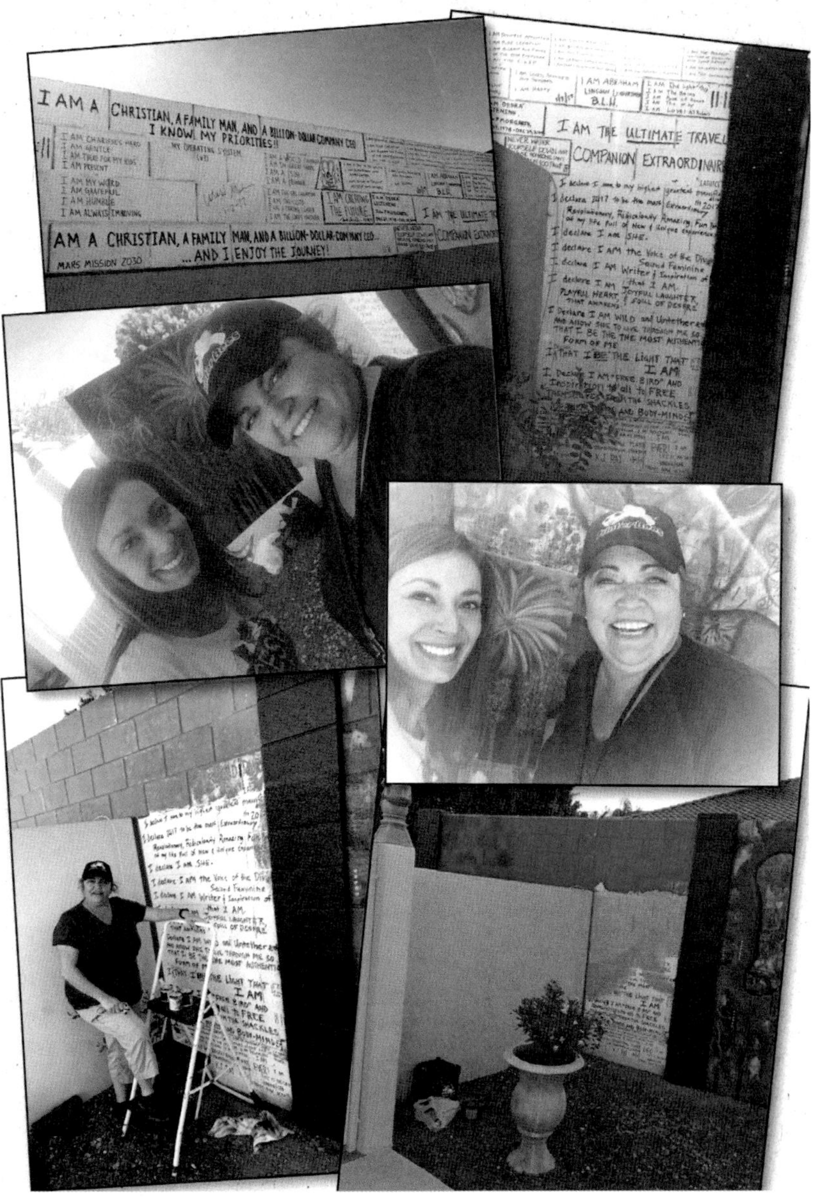

4-4-2017

Love these photos of Gina "Shakti" right where her powerful declarations are below the surface of "The Matriarch." Steve added one last loving note and I'm always happy to see Amy!

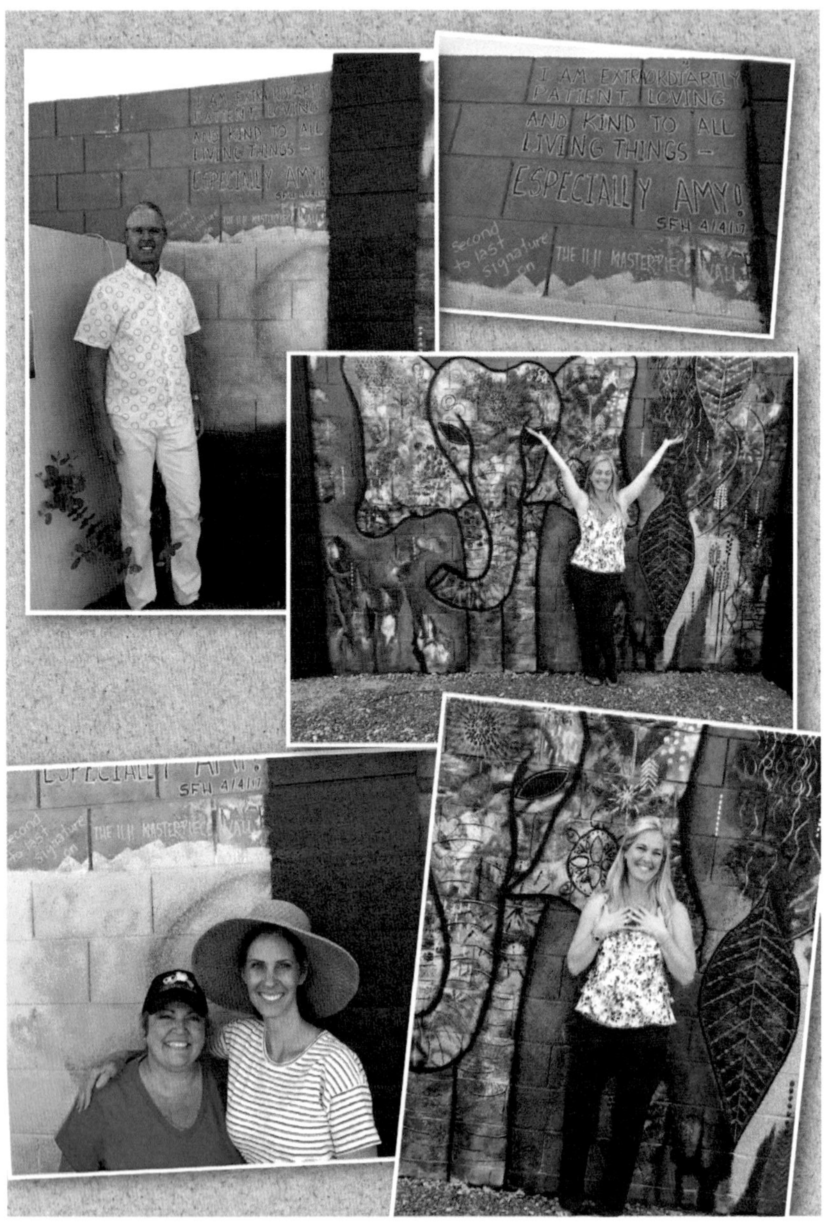

4-5-2017

My favorite photos are the ones that I receive via text from Steve in the morning. The sun lights up the wall as it progresses forward. I love… love… love the angel photo.

4-5-2017

Today I stayed late to trace the phoenix shape on to the wall. Steve had fun as the camera man!

4-6-2017

Today was a challenge. I struggled with the shape of the bird/ phoenix and the wings. Steve was so helpful and supportive. I'm so appreciative, I've never known anyone like him. And… It's always so great to see John Vehr.

4-7-2017

I got past my frustration with trying to get the shape of the wings and the body correct and I'm now progressing forward. I felt pretty challenged and frustrated yesterday. Glad I kept at it and didn't give up.

4-11-2017

Today I completed "Phoenix Rising!" It feels so good to keep progressing forward. It's on to the clouds next!

4-11-2017

This is the first time I've ever painted clouds. I wasn't pleased with my first attempt and ended up painting over it so I could start over. Edward Olaya with the painting Steve and I gifted to he and Abigail's triplets.

4-12-2017

A fresh start to attempt clouds on the wall. I practiced on a small canvas before coming to paint today to see if that would help me get the hang of it. Onward!!!

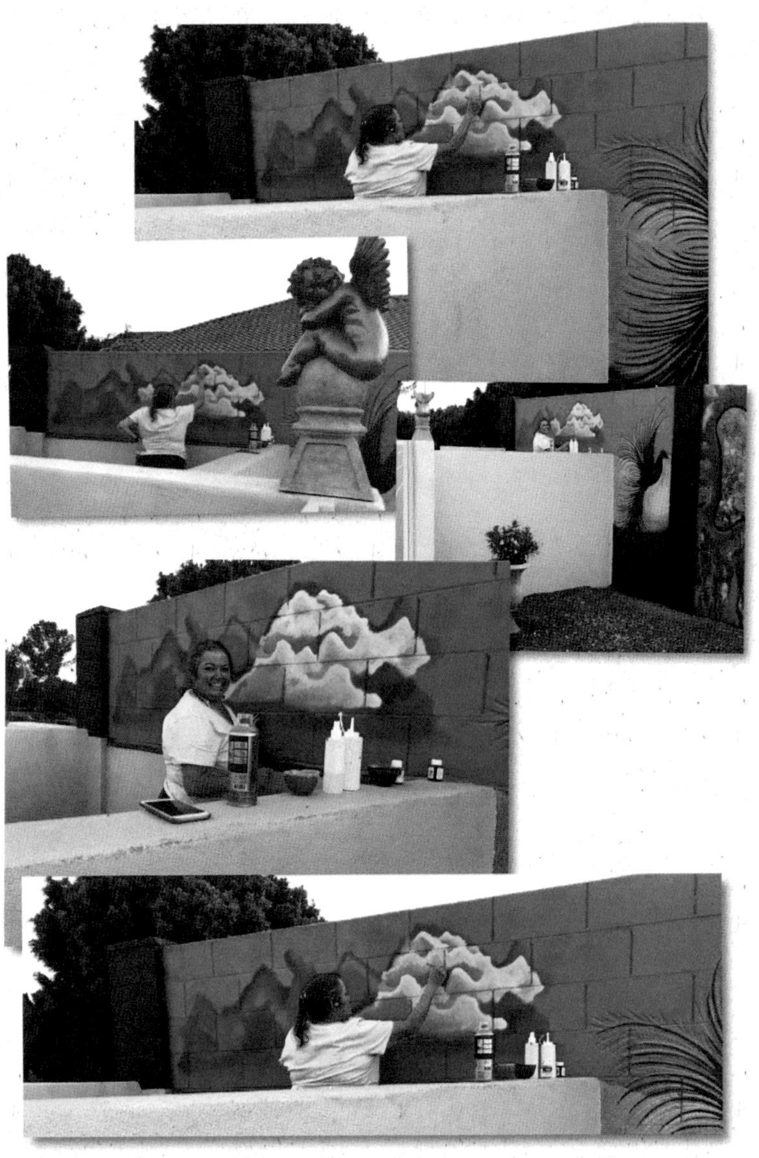

4-13-2017

I've got my head in the clouds...

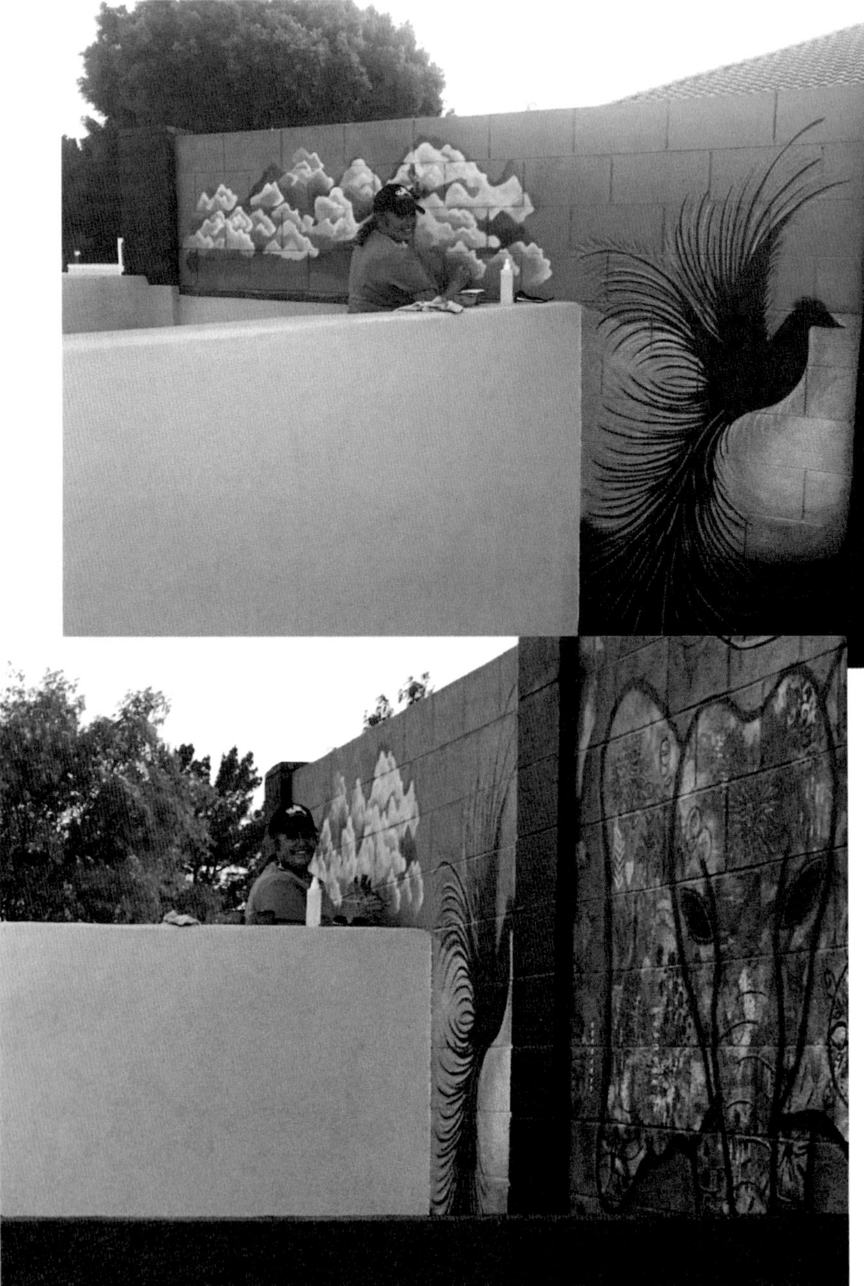

4-14-2017

I'm making great progress on my clouds and they look like clouds! So proud of myself considering I've never done clouds before.

4-17-2017

This day was tooooo fun! Steve decided it would be fun to hang out with me while I painted my clouds. LOL

4-17-2017

Steve "auditioning" some letters on the pillars of the wall to see how it might look if I painted "I Am that I Am" on them. I've seriously had so much fun doing this project.

4-17-2017

The clouds next to "Phoenix Rising" are complete! Yay! So proud of myself for accomplishing this. The entire front side of the wall is done! I'm blown away!

4-19-2017

Getting started on "Powerhouse," the last mural to complete The 11:11 Masterpiece Wall. I continue to be in awe of the entire process and that I'm actually doing this. It's crazy… crazy good!

4-20-2017

Adding more layers of paint to "Powerhouse" and I'm loving all the bright contrasting colors.

4-24-2017

I couldn't have been more excited or proud to have my daughter Alyssa come to town with Nicole and Allie and have them see the wall in person. They loved it! A really proud moment for me. Their first time seeing it in person.

5-3-2017

After a week off to spend time with my kids, I'm back at it. Working on "Powerhouse." Steve was here to greet me! So fun to be back at "the wall" doing my art!

5-4-2017

"Powerhouse" is taking shape and looking like the African Queen she is. I'm loving her! OMGosh!

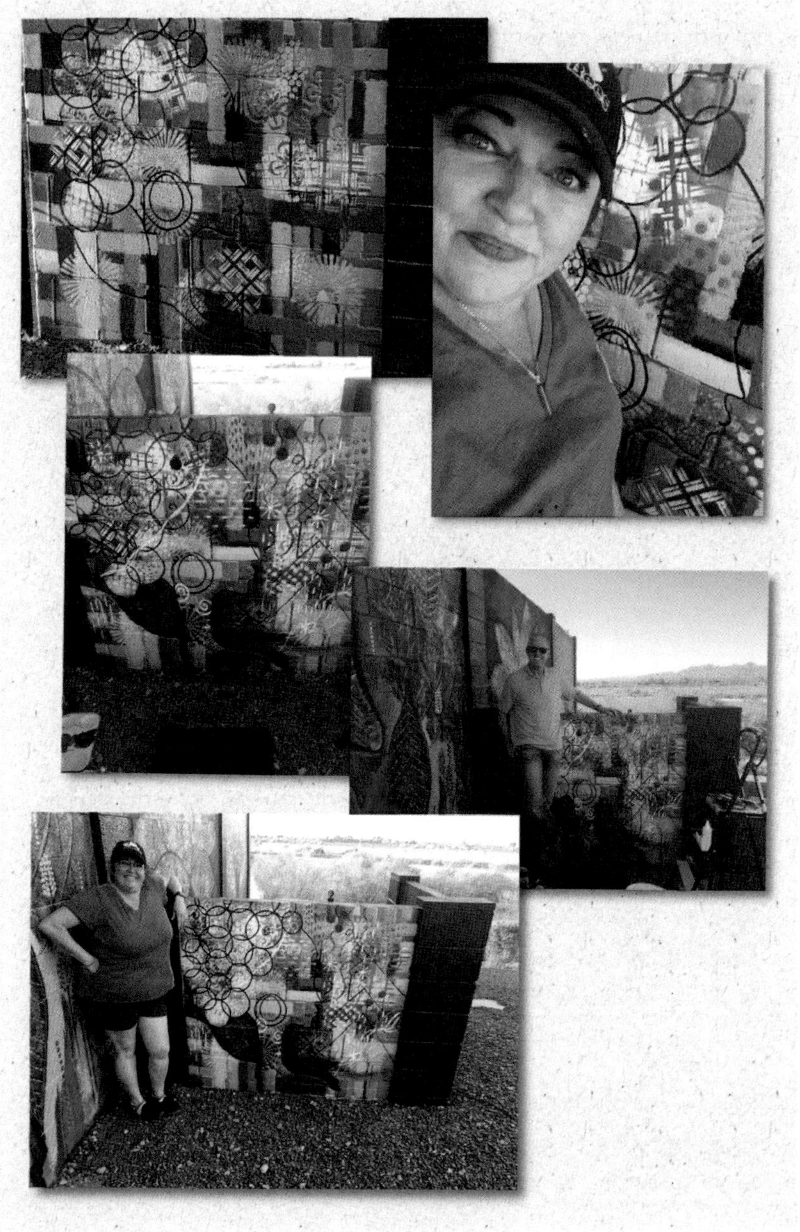

5-8-2017

I'm getting so close to being done and I love the way "Powerhouse" looks as I get closer to completing her.

5-9-2017

Powerhouse is complete!!! Feel so proud to have painted all these murals.

5-10-2017

The final step in completing The 11:11 Masterpiece Wall is "The Lotus Pond." We wanted to tie the inside wall where the pool equipment is in to the lotus right next to it, so we made it a lotus pond! This is it! One last part to complete and this masterpiece will be done. I can't believe I did it!

5-12-2017

Received photos from Steve of Clara next to the wall she wrote her "Powerhouse" declaration on. Her declaration was the inspiration for the name of this painting. Love seeing her next to this wall.

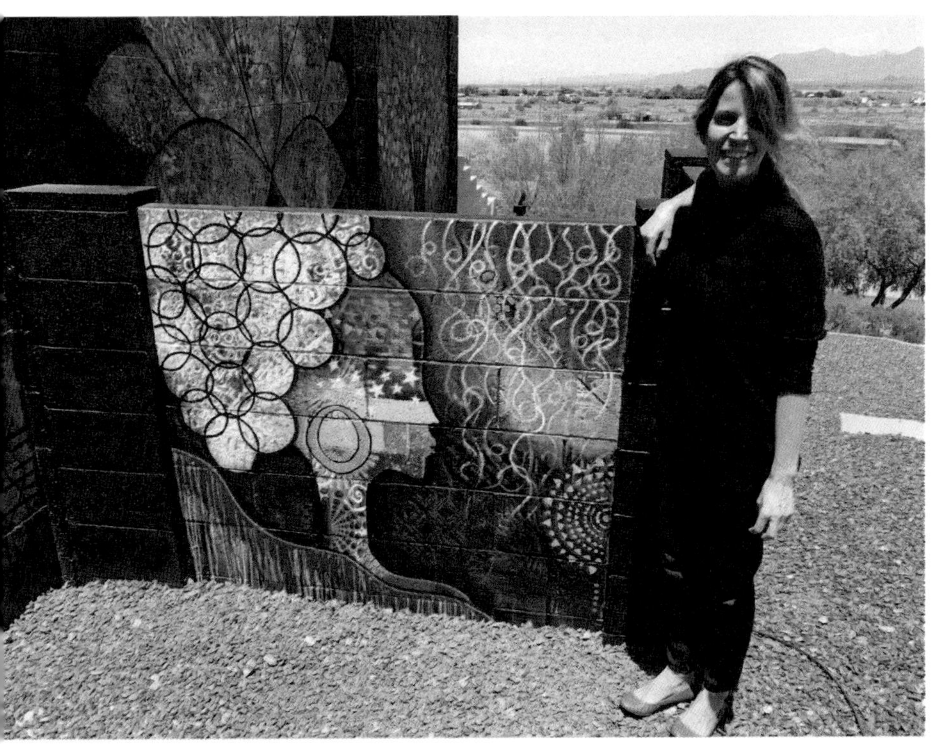

5-15-2017

I'm back at it… completing the lotus pond and enjoying all the bright colors of these lotus flowers. Feeling happy and sad at the same time, knowing my time with Steve and Amy Hardison is nearing an end as I get closer and closer to completing this amazing project.

5-16-2017

These lotus flowers are looking great if you ask me! I think after painting all these walls, my confidence has finally arrived to help me along! LOL Better late than never.

5-17-2017

Today I had my mind blown when the "lighting guys" came to demonstrate how my art would look with spotlights on it. I was gifted the most beautiful bouquet as thank you from Steve and Amy for my work. There's only touch up and the pool pump left to complete.

5-20-2017

It was exactly two years ago today that I picked up a paint brush for the first time. I had no idea I could create art two years ago. If someone would have told me that I would be painting and completing a 600 sq. ft. mural exactly two years later, I would have told them they were crazy. It's amazing what we can do when we put our mind to doing it and believe it can be done. I'm so incredibly proud of myself for taking on this project. I'm incredibly thankful to Steve and Amy for believing in me that I could do it. Something I had never done before but had faith in my ability to learn as I went along.

Today I completed this amazing project with the love and support of my husband, my children, my family, my business, my friends, my faith in God, lots of prayer and meditation, the 444 people who's name are on the wall, the power and energy of the declarations below the surface and Steve and Amy Hardison. I will forever be grateful for this life

changing project. The project of a lifetime. The 11:11 Masterpiece Wall.

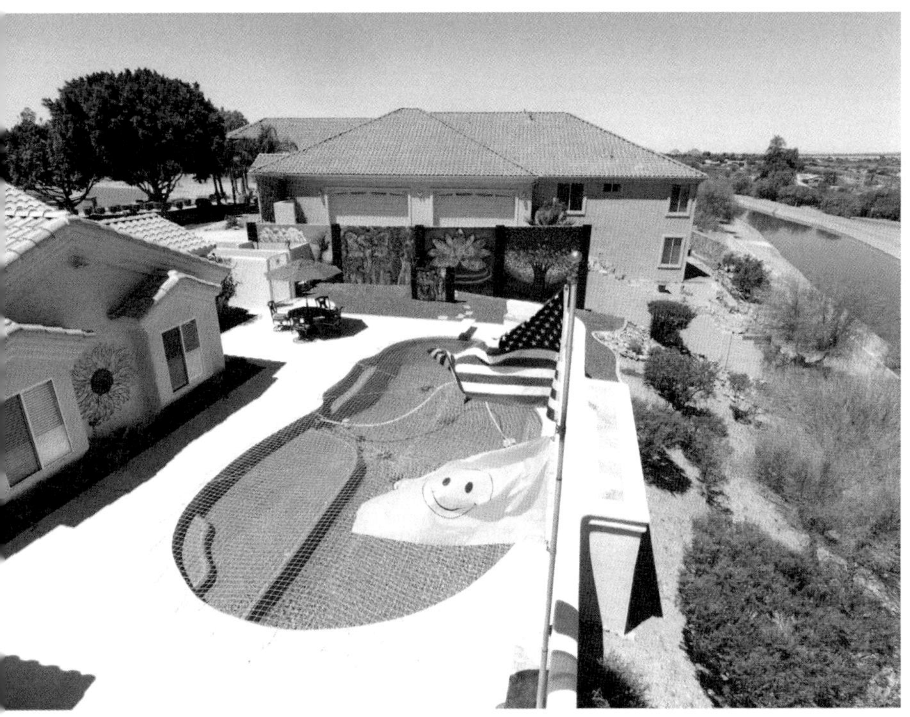

The yellow flag flying on the flag pole is the flag that flew when I was coaching with Steve. Every client has their own flag that flies when they are there for coaching. I loved seeing my flag fly high the day I completed the wall.

5-20-2017

Photos from my last day.

The end…

For information regarding Nadine J. Larder, visit:

www.NadineLarder.com

If you enjoyed this book, you might also enjoy the other books in this series.

The Secrets I Share With My Friends
Life Lessons From An Imperfect Woman
Available On Kindle

The Secrets I Share With My Friends
Everything I Know About Building A Small Business
Available in Paperback on Amazon

Made in the USA
Coppell, TX
01 August 2021